Assessment through Interviewing

SECOND EDITION

BY

GEORGE SHOUKSMITH

Department of Psychology
Massey University, New Zealand

PERGAMON PRESS
Oxford · New York · Toronto · Sydney · Paris · Frankfurt

U. K.	Pergamon Press Ltd., Headington Hill Hall, Oxford OX3 0BW, England
U. S. A.	Pergamon Press Inc., Maxwell House, Fairview Park, Elmsford, New York 10523, U.S.A.
CANADA	Pergamon of Canada Ltd., 75 The East Mall, Toronto, Ontario, Canada
AUSTRALIA	Pergamon Press (Aust.) Pty. Ltd., 19a Boundary Street, Rushcutters Bay, N.S.W. 2011, Australia
FRANCE	Pergamon SARL, 24 rue des Ecoles, 75240 Paris, Cedex 05, France
FEDERAL REPUBLIC OF GERMANY	Pergamon Press GmbH, 6242 Kronberg-Taunus Pferdstrasse 1, Federal Republic of Germany

Copyright © 1978 George Shouksmith

First edition 1968

Second edition 1978

British Library Cataloguing in Publication Data
Shouksmith, George
Assessment through interviewing. – 2nd ed.
1. Employment interviewing
I. Title
658.31'12   HF5549.5.16   77-30489
ISBN 0-08-021152-6 (Hardcover)
ISBN 0-09-021151-8 (Flexicover)

Printed in Great Britain by A. Wheaton & Co. Ltd., Exeter

PERGAMON I N   R A R Y
of Science, Techr ology, Engineering and Social Studies
The 1000-volume original paperback library in aid of education,
industrial training and the enjoyment of leisure
Publisher: Robert Maxwell, M.C.

Assess   **Bristol**
            Polytechnic
S E C O N
             Author: SHOUKSMITH

             Title: Assessment through interview

             This book should be returned by the
             te st ured below

THE PERGAMON TEXTBOOK
INSPECTION COPY SERVICE

An inspection copy of any book published in the Pergamon International Library will
gladly be sent to academic staff without obligation for their consideration for course
adoption or recommendation. Copies may be retained for a period of 60 days from
receipt and returned if not suitable. When a particular title is adopted or recommended
for adoption for class use and the recommendation results in a sale of 12 or more copies,
the inspection copy may be retained with our compliments. The Publishers will be
pleased to receive suggestions for revised editions and new titles to be published in this
important International Library.

Some Other Titles of Interest

DuBRIN, A.J.
The Fundamentals of Organizational Behavior

DuBRIN, A.J.
The Practice of Managerial Psychology

HUGHES, F.W.
Human Relations in Management

JOYCE, R.D.
Encounters in Organizational Behavior: Problem Situations

KANFER, F.H. & GOLDSTEIN, A.P.
Helping People Change: A Textbook of Methods

MORRICE, J.K.W.
Crisis Intervention — Studies in Community Care

MOSES, J.L.
Applying the Assessment Center Method

SINGER, G. & WALLACE, M.
The Administrative Waltz

Contents

Preface to the Second Edition

The use and practice of interviewing in selection and other assessment situations was the focal point of the first edition of this book and remains so in the second edition. Changes in this edition are introduced mainly to up-date basic material. I have used the first edition for a text for innumerable courses on assessment interviewing held both in the United Kingdom and in New Zealand. It has proved to be a very useful handbook for guiding teachers, university students, industrial and commercial managers, and public servants through these courses, and in practice. The second edition retains, therefore, the basic material and format of the first. From follow-up evaluations of the training programmes in which it was used, however, certain needs for expanding the material were revealed. This edition includes extended material on planning for the interview and on the conduct of the interview, aimed at making its coverage of the basic concerns more comprehensive. Use of groups for individual assessment and development, particularly in human relations training contexts, has increased immeasurably in the late sixties and early seventies. It seemed appropriate, therefore, to give a more extensive treatment of the theory and practice of group dynamics so as to round off the whole picture. Finally, both research and practice in the use of the interview therapeutically have advanced over the past few years, and so the use of counselling interviews receives somewhat more attention in this edition than it did in the last.

Many colleagues and friends have helped develop my thinking about interviewing through providing feedback on their use of the book and by contributing to teaching programmes and seminars based on the text. My thanks are expressed to them, particularly those in the Department of Psychology at Massey University and those friends in N.A.C., Braith Hyde and Don French, who have helped me to relate theory and practice. My thanks also go to Mrs. Joan Judd for her patience and efficiency in typing this second edition of the Handbook.

PART I

Practising Individual Interviewing

C H A P T E R 1

The Nature of the Interview

There is a very real sense in which it can be said that there is no such thing as the interview but that there are many interviews. The personnel officer brings a candidate into his office to assess his suitability for a particular job; the teacher passes on to parents information about their son's or daughter's progress; the doctor tries to help a patient by sorting out some of his troubles: all are engaged in interviewing in one form or another. Interviewing can be used in many different ways and for many different ends, and each kind of interview has its own methods and characteristics.

There are selection and placement interviews used by managers and executives to choose staff; there are vocational guidance interviews, counselling interviews to help the emotionally disturbed, and survey interviews used by market researchers; then there are the various forms of group interviewing, used for problem solving, assessment, or therapy, and diagnostic interviews used by clinical psychologists. More recently, organizational psychologists have introduced into industry appraisal interviews linked to participative management programmes and organizational development. Exit interviews have been introduced for staff leaving, and attitude change programmes have been used to motivate existing staff and increase their job satisfaction. There seems no end to the diversity of uses in which the face-to-face encounter we call the interview can be employed.

Even within any one type of interview there is by no means only one method. Selection interviews can be conducted by a Board or an individual, and counselling interviews may be psychoanalytic or nondirective in orientation according to the beliefs of the counsellor. All these differences adding to the varied nature of interviewing have made many people critical of interviews, particularly those concerned with assessment. Critics point to the lack of standardization and maintain that because of this the interview must of necessity be unreliable. But in one sense the very lack of standardization in the interview is its major strength as well as its major weakness. If, for example, we compare an interview with a psychological test this will become clear. A psychological test is a standardized measuring instrument, but its application is limited to the type of person and the type of situation for which it was prepared. Once you transfer to another situation and test some other kind of person with it, then it immediately loses value as a measuring instrument. The interview, on the other hand, has the supreme advantage of flexibility, so that with slight modification it can be used in any set of circumstances. It also has the advantage of flexibility in another sense. Whereas the test measures one or two aspects of a person only, the interview can be used to get a global picture of a whole individual. Furthermore, there are few if any personality tests which can validly be used in industrial or commercial settings, so that the interview remains the only practical method of assessing personality.

Since the interview has advantages and in some respects unique possibilities, it would seem ridiculous to deny its use completely merely because it is unstandardized and because some interviews are of little value. A more sensible approach would be to attempt to isolate and consolidate good interviewing. The problem is to produce a reliable and valid technique without losing flexibility. As Bass (1968) points out: "The interview presents a particular challenge to the personnel and social psychologist, for no matter what can or cannot be demonstrated about its utility as an assessment device, it is almost universal in use for selection purposes." From a practical viewpoint it would seem best, therefore, to use our psychological research findings and technology to make our assessment interviews as good and effective as possible.

One difficulty faces us in any attempts we make to achieve this aim. Many people like to think that they are naturally good at interviewing. It is consequently difficult to persuade them of the need for improvement in their interviewing techniques or of the possibility that their interviewing and the assessments they derive from interviews could possibly be improved by training. The worst offender is the self-styled natural expert who tells me: "Of course, I'm pretty good at summing a man up myself. They only have to be in the room for a few minutes and I get the measure of them. I always say either you are born a good interviewer or you are not."

Firstly, he is the one who may well arrive at biased conclusions based on initial perceptions which may well be irrelevant to the assessment task in hand. Secondly, he is unlikely to accept any criticism of his own skills or techniques and thus never improve. In demonstrable truth, however, not only can interviewing be improved by training — and even the odd interviewer who was not "born", be "made" by training — but even the best interviewer has faults which, however minor, can be corrected. A colleague of mine who was one of the most painstaking and thorough interviewers I have known, once admitted that he had found himself biasing his interview assessments of any candidate who wore a hacking jacket. Completely irrationally, he just could not stand people wearing flaps at the back of their jackets, and until he realized this he was, subconsciously almost, marking down anyone who appeared in such a dress. The assessment one makes can easily be biased by prejudices. One of those people who was a "born interviewer" once admitted that the first thing he looked at in a candidate was the school tie. He had certain preferences which rightly or wrongly would bias his judgement. A prejudice may lead you in the right direction but equally it might not. Your judgement of a person will remain biased until you either erase these prejudices from your mind or at least recognize and control them. Such biases lead to unreliability in the interview. Technically, "reliability" refers to the consistency of measurement. If a measure of anything is not consistent, varies according to who makes the measure, and so on, it can hardly be a useful measure. An interview which cannot be relied upon to give the same answer on two or more occasions is hardly a suitable tool for personnel assessment.

Hollingworth as early as 1929 (Hollingworth, 1929) made the serious criticism of interviews that compared with standardized tests they were woefully prone to inconsistent appraisals. He quotes an investigation in which 12 sales managers interviewed 57 prospective employees. The results, to quote Hollingworth, show that "any given applicant is likely to receive ratings placing him at any point in the scale from first position to last. Applicant C, for example, is given position 1 by one judge, 57 by another, 2 by a third, and 53 by a fourth . . .": at first sight a complete condemnation of the interview. One must remember, however, that interviewing techniques have had a chance to improve since the twenties, and, moreover, even the data collected by Hollingworth is not as clear-cut as it appears at first sight. Laird (1937), for example, has pointed out that in reworking the original data he discovered that although there were large discrepancies throughout, some pairs of sales managers had rating lists which correlated as highly as 0.83. Thus a better conclusion would appear to be merely that some people make reliable interviewers and others do not. This, however, raises the second point that if some interviewers can produce reliable assessments there is room for improvement and a need for a clear analysis of what produces such reliability.

Hunt *et al.* (1944), in a report on the use of the interview for psychiatric screening in the services, give one clue as to a possible source of unreliability. When psychiatrists were asked to place recruits into detailed specific personality categories they achieved only 32% agreement as to the designation of particular recruits. When broad categories were used, however, agreement rose to 54%, and when only two categories — "fit" or "unfit" for service — were used, agreement was as high as 95%. We can learn one lesson from this and that is that the unreliability is produced by asking the interview to do too much — to discriminate more finely than it is capable of doing.

To be useful the assessment interview must not only be reliable but also valid. The interview's validity is a measure of the extent to which it does measure accurately what it sets out to measure — in selection work its accuracy in predicting whether a candidate will succeed in the position or job he is applying for. The findings regarding validity tend to be as confusing as those regarding reliability. North American psychologists long ago grew sceptical of the interview as a selection device. Kelly and Fiske (1951), as representative American researchers of some standing, quote higher validities for objective tests alone than for a combination of tests plus interview. On the other hand, Vernon (1950), working in the United Kingdom, referring to the new Civil Service Selection Boards, reports that no test has anywhere near as high a validity as the interview. If one looks more closely at the various investigations of interview validity; what emerges is that results differ according to the situation in which the interview is used. In predicting aptitude for tradesmen jobs in the British Army, tests were found to be of higher value alone than when interviews were added to the selection (Vernon and Parry, 1949). At the executive level of the Civil Service Selection Boards, as we have already seen, the reverse was true. What emerges is that there appear to be some situations where the interview is not a relevant assessment tool, and in these situations any predictions made from interviews are likely to be of low validity.

More sophisticated modern interviewing techniques appear to improve the picture as one recent comprehensive study of interviewing demonstrates. Grant and Bray (1969) report findings from a major practical assessment interviewing programme involving 348 men involved in the Bell System Management Progress Study. "The findings of this study suggest", Grant and Bray report, "that the interview may have considerable scope and still be reliable and valid." The study demonstrates that the interview can vary in reliability according to the variables being assessed and the socio-educational status of the group being interviewed. Assessments over some 18 variables made by a team of 6 interviewers varied in reliability from 0.73 to 0.92 as measured by intercorrelation coefficients, with a median reliability of 0.82 when these assessments were made on college graduate members of the programme. Assessments made of non-graduate members of the programme produced a median reliability of only 0.72 and showed a much wider spread of individual reliabilities over the whole 18 variables. The study also showed that the validity of assessments varied according to the quality or aspect of the individual being assessed — some things are more readily assessed by the interview than others. In the study, for example, the assessment interviews had high concurrent validity — measured in terms of correlations with other independent assessments of the variables concerned — for the assessment of underlying career motivation, interpersonal skill characteristics of the interviewee, and a number of subsidiary interpersonal and motivational variables.

It seems clear that the assessment task, or type of judgement the interviewer has to make, will affect both the reliability and validity of the interview. Carlson *et al.* (1971), in a major and generally critical survey of assessment interviewing, point to task variation as one of four factors affecting the decision making of the assessment interviewer. The other three are the physical and psychological properties of (a) the interviewee and (b) the interviewer, and the general situational factors within which the interviewer works. In this they follow Symonds' (1939) earlier studies which indicated that three sets of factors may influence the reliability and validity of interviews. These are:

(1) Factors within the applicant, such as age, sex, intelligence, race, cultural and socio-economic group, linguistic ability, emotional stability, needs and attitudes, and possibly his previous experience of assessment interviews.

(2) Factors within the interviewer, including his age, sex, intelligence, and social group, but also including his personality and social warmth, his depth of psychological understanding, and also his authority position.

(3) Factors in the general situation, including the physical environment of the interview, its duration and time of day, the interviewee's experiences immediately prior to the interview, etc.

The postulation that there are these three sets of factors influencing interviewing assessments, recognizes that the interview is an interpersonal interaction situation. In the face-to-face interview there are two people involved and both will influence its outcome as will both their reactions to the general situation in which the interview takes place. A good interviewer will, of course, determine the pattern of interactions which emerges. If he is a good interviewer the pattern of the interview will be under his control. To achieve this control the interviewer will not necessarily direct the pattern of interactions rigidly since he wants the interviewee to reveal those dominant behavioural and attitude patterns which are important to him. The interviewer's role is to create a natural conversation flow or interaction pattern which, nevertheless, remains task-relevant, so that his judgements are not biased by irrelevant observations.

Carlson *et al.* (1971), suggest that inexperienced interviewers are most likely to be influenced in this way. General research in psychology tells us that experience without feedback as to its effectiveness is of little value, which underlines the need for interview-training programmes where, perhaps, using videotape, an interviewer can assess his own good and bad points and modify his techniques accordingly. Carlson *et. al.* also suggest two further areas which are important in helping the interviewer use the interview situation effectively. Firstly, they agree that a structured interview is better than an unstructured one. It is true that a totally unstructured interview is of little value – the interaction process loses direction and in all probability no assessment is made. A completely structured interview, where the interviewer uses a set list of unvaried questions, would no doubt raise the reliability of the assessment but would not enhance the validity of the personal assessments made and would remove one of the interview's major assets — its flexibility. Grant and Bray's research (1969) possibly indicates one effective method of structuring. Their interviewers were provided with personal biographical information about the interviewee before the interview took place. The interviewer reviewed this information in preparation for the interview and from it isolated areas for probing during the interview, these areas being chosen as likely to throw light on the 18 variables being assessed, which themselves were carefully predefined. Carlson's final point referred to the need for some standardization of the evaluation system, so that the large amount of information generated by the interview can be reduced and directed towards assessment of a manageable number of constant dimensions. Grant and Bray's interviewers were all highly skilled and experienced, yet, even so, only some of the variables they used could be reliably assessed. For most general purposes a much smaller set of predefined assessment categories would seem desirable. The Grant and Bray study, however, does show the effectiveness of having predetermined assessment categories, isolated before the interview, so that they can aid the structuring of the interview itself.

These arguments may be summed up by three simple points which together isolate the major factors on which to a large degree the usefulness of the interview depends.

Firstly, the importance of excluding or controlling bias in assessments emerges. The competent interviewer is one who knows his own biases and whose interview technique is such that it excludes bias as much as possible from the assessment.

Secondly, the interview can become highly unreliable as an assessment tool in certain circumstances. This it does, for example, when asked to distinguish too finely. You should not, therefore, ask too much of the interview. From the research findings it also emerges that some judgement tasks are more suited to assessment through the interview than others, and so assessments in those areas tend to be more reliable and, indeed, more valid.

Thirdly, this finding that in some situations the interview is not valid raises the whole question of the relevance of interviewing. Before using an interview you must ask always, Is it relevant in this situation?

Relevance is a two-sided thing. To know whether the interview is a relevant assessment tool you must also know exactly what it is you want to assess; know the relevant qualities or traits which, for example, an applicant must have. Only if you know these can you say whether through the interview you can assess them. Bingham and Moore (1959) define the interview as a "conversation with a purpose". The conversation you hold in the interview must have a specific and relevant purpose which then helps to direct the course of the conversation.

When two people interact, their conversation may take many forms, few of these being relevant to the sort of assessment problem the interviewer is faced with. Therefore the interviewer is called upon somehow to direct the interaction flow towards the achievement of a certain goal — the assessment of certain predetermined qualities. The interactions should become limited to that area which is concerned with this goal or task. How well the interactions deal with the task depends to a large extent on the interviewer's skills. Beyond this, however, lies the fundamental necessity of isolating for any interview programme a specific task or goal which can be used by the interviewer to guide him as to the direction of the interaction process we call the interview.

CHAPTER 2

What to Assess

If we are concerned with selection or assessment interviewing the first thing we must establish is what it is we want to assess. The interaction process must be directed so as to throw light on those particular facets of the individual candidates which are important for the position being considered. If the interview is being used to choose a man to be a foreman, then you must ask what are the characteristics of a good foreman in this trade and in this firm. It is no use wasting the time of candidate or interviewer discussing things which have no relevance at all to the job for which the candidate is being considered. Such undirected interaction can only lead to the interviewer's biases and prejudices coming to the fore. If the interviewer has no clear idea of how interaction should be directed, no clear idea of what aspects of the candidate's personality he is supposed to assess, then the conversation will tend to follow, in the case of a strong candidate, his interests, or more likely and more frequently, the fads, fancies, interests, and concerns of the interviewer. The interview is a conversation with a purpose, the purpose or task serving to guide or direct the interaction pattern or conversation. The nature of the task determines whether the interview is a relevant assessment tool to use — and we have seen that it is more relevant to the assessment of certain personal attributes than it is in the case of others. The personal factors whose qualities can be assessed in human beings through an interview determine the general task or purpose of the interview. In any one interview not all of these would be relevant to the task in hand. Hence a further limited listing of characteristics desired or essential in applicants for a particular job would be needed to form the specific task or purpose of a selection interview. Similarly, in assessment of existing staff for promotion or in annual appraisal, the interviewer requires a list of personal attributes relevant to the interviewee's job situation which tell the interviewer what he is looking for.

The General Purposes of Interviewing

Not everything that one wants to know about a job candidate can be adequately assessed through the interview. Anstey and Mercer (1956), for example, identify seven general descriptive areas which can be used in the assessment of any job applicant, these areas being derived from the descriptive categories used in Rodger's (1952) seven-point plan. These assessment areas describe the applicant in terms of:

(1) His knowledge in terms of:
   (a) general educational level, and (b) special knowledge or skills in job area.
(2) His general ability or intelligence (capacity for learning as opposed to what he has learned).
(3) Evidence of any special aptitudes.
(4) Disposition as shown in (a) effectiveness with others — human relations, and (b) effectiveness in work — drive, energy, care, etc.
(5) His aims and interests in relation to the work situation.
(6) His physical capacities.
(7) His opportunities and the use he has made of them.

Of these 1(a) and (2) may best be assessed through formal examinations by using standardized tests or by reference to appropriate records. Some researchers in interviewing claim that ability or intelligence can be assessed through the interview. It seems likely that general ability may be being confused with verbal ability, however, as there are many intelligent backroom boys who lack general communications skills and so show up badly in the interview. Some aspects of 1(b) may be available for assessment through the interview, for example, by assessing the quality of previous experience or by requiring the interviewee to display these skills through the medium of a technical conversation. Other aspects may best be assessed by trying out the· applicant in a real or simulated job task or by using an objective and standardized ·test. The same remarks apply in general to area (3). Areas (4) and (5) are difficult to assess in any case. A variety of methods have been developed for assessing these qualities, many of which are only available to a qualified clinical psychologist. Thus for most practical everyday purposes these factors are best assessed by the individual or group interview. Area (6) ˙can certainly be assessed in part through the interview, though where physical standards are critical a thorough medical examination is more appropriate. Area (7), too, is suitable for partial assessment through the interview providing we remember that the "factual" statements an applicant makes about life are all coloured by his own self-image and viewpoints on life. What is revealed through the interview is not a series of facts but rather the impressions of a live human being. The interview reveals what he thinks and feels about his experiences of life, how he sees himself, the aims and ambitions he is prepared to reveal to the world, and his views about jobs and life in general. What also emerges is a partial picture at least of his competence in social situations of which the interview is one. The general purposes for which the interview can be used are, therefore, limited. In summary, the interviewer can expect to obtain most reliable and valid information about the following characteristics of the interviewee:

(1) His appearance and general manner.
(2) His verbal and other interpersonal skills.
(3) Some other skills and attainments in areas where the interviewer has special knowledge.
(4) His revealed attitudes to jobs, other persons, and his experiences of life.
(5) His sociability, interpersonal and social behaviour.

(6) Limited aspects of his motivational drive and energy.
(7) His emotional make-up and possible degree of stability.
(8) His personal maturity, clarity of self-image.
(9) His aspirations.

Naturally, only the most experienced and expert interviewer will be competent over the full range of these. The "deeper" the personal quality the more difficult it is to assess but often the more important. The beginning interviewer does best to keep to the simpler aspects in his early days of experience, extending his assessments only as he begins to get the "feel" of interviewing. Again, the importance is underlined of practical experience training with appropriate feedback to enable the interviewer to extend his assessments over the full range of tasks for which the interview is generally suited.

The Special Purposes of an Interview

Not all these areas for which the interview can provide information are likely to be relevant to a specific assessment situation. We require some technique for isolating the specific goal or task for each assessment problem. Unless the interviewer knows exactly what he is looking for, the interaction becomes undirected, the conversation without purpose, and thus, one might argue, no longer truly an interview.

We have seen that one of the sources of unreliability in interviewing is bias. If we have in front of us a list of factors which we are to assess in the interview, then these can prevent us from letting our own prejudices come to the fore by keeping our minds on the essentials. Furthermore, the possession of such a guide in the formulation of what the specific task is ensures that our conversation will be relevant. Thus at the outset, before beginning the actual interviewing of candidates, a list must be produced of the critical requirements for the job in question. This list will then act as a guide in directing the conversation in the interview to relevant topics only.

In selection interviewing you are concerned with predicting

whether a certain candidate would, if you gave him the chance, make a success of a particular job. In order to do this you must first know what sort of person will make a success of that job. And it is not sufficient merely to know this in some general way. What is wanted is a detailed knowledge of the factors, traits and qualities in a human being which lead to success in that job. These are what Flanagan (1947) has called the "critical requirements" for that job. In order to produce these critical requirements, however, you must first obtain a detailed analysis of the job in terms of the person in the job. This analysis covers all the facets of the job: the background of the job, the sort of training a person needs for it, the aptitudes, attainments, type of personality, character, or temperament required. All the significant and insignificant, large and small factors involved in doing the job, all the characteristics inherited and acquired of the kind of person who succeeds at this job, are detailed in the job analysis. From this detailed and complete statement are isolated the few critical factors or features which can be said to be of supreme importance in producing success or failure in the job.

Why not merely use the detailed analysis? Firstly, it would in the normal half-hour to hour interview, or even in a much longer period, be impossible to cover the whole of the job analysis. Secondly, it is also well beyond the powers of even the most intelligent and capable human being to be able to match a live person against all the factors in such a complete and detailed job analysis. Such a task would require some sort of electronic computer. Interviewers are rarely the most capable of human beings, let alone computers. So to simplify the task we reduce our full analysis to a set of critical requirements. Four or five, or at the most six, critical and relevant factors to consider is not beyond the capability of the normal person and so makes a much better and more practical task for the interviewer. This approach ties in with the finding that when asked to distinguish too finely the interview's reliability and validity diminishes. In using a few "critical requirements" rather than the whole job analysis we hope to raise the value of the interview assessment by limiting the area for assessment.

Job Analysis

A job analysis is defined by Roger Bellows in his textbook on industrial psychology (1961) as: "an orderly and systematic study of the characteristics, duties, and responsibilities of a specific job." Providing the study is made systematically and providing the analysis gives the information about the job in terms of the person who is to do it, then it does not really matter how the analysis is made. There are many methods of producing job analyses: which one you use can depend largely on your own inclinations. Two important considerations must always be kept in mind, however. Your analysis must be something more than an armchair affair. In making an analysis you should, whenever possible, observe the job being done, talk to the various people concerned with the job, and discuss with them the various aspects of the job and their implications. Furthermore, your analysis, when made, should be checked with competent and independent officials and against the appropriate trade or professional standards.

Three examples of classification schemes forming a job analysis are given below. The first two approach the task in somewhat different ways. The third is an extended form of analysis which is essentially a combination of the first two. All three of these techniques basically consist of looking at the job in terms of a number of headings. The headings ensure that a systematic appraisal is made and that by following a set plan you miss nothing out. Although some occupations require the more detailed analysis and others are, by their nature, marginally more suited to one method or the other, in general the choice is largely one of personal preference.

Job Analysis: Method 1

1. TITLE. A definitive title identifying the job exactly, is given.
   DUTIES. A general description is given first and then a detailed breakdown of the duties involved is given under the following headings:

(a) *Skill.* The planning, decision making, judgement, etc., which the job requires.

(b) *Effort.* The physical and mental demands made on the individual. Questions of the need for alertness or concentration are considered here.

(c) *Responsibility.* This section considers the responsibilities inherent in the job. Responsibilities for material or equipment or supervisory responsibilities for the work or safety of others.

2. JOB CONDITIONS. A statement should be given of the physical working conditions together with any special features of the job; e.g. particular hazards. The conditions of the job will always suit some people and not others, so that a statement of what these are is important for selection work.

3. QUALIFICATIONS

(a) *Educational.* Schooling level, i.e. school certificate etc., and any other formal training or certificates required, e.g. university degree, technical college diploma.

(b) *Training.* The background specialist training required which may vary from short-term on the job training through apprenticeships to internships following formal education.

(c) *Experience.* In some jobs or occupations, previous experience in a junior position is essential. This should be stated and the importance of this experience in the fulfilment of the job as a whole indicated.

4. POSITION AND PROSPECTS. A job may offer promotion prospects or it may not. Its present position may be of high or low status and these factors are all required to give a complete picture of the job. Also in this final section it is useful to note the relationship of the job being studied to other positions, branches, and departments of the firm.

Although this system does consider the person, one possible drawback is that its emphasis is on the job itself rather than the person in the job. For this reason, my own preference is for the second technique which aims at describing not so much the job itself as the person who can successfully tackle the particular job. This technique, like Anstey and Mercer's analysis of job factors, is based on Alec Rodger's seven-point plan (1952). The idea of the plan was to assess people's prospects for particular jobs in terms of seven points. This plan could be used in selection work or guidance, the assessor or counsellor taking each of the seven points in turn and checking the demands of the job under that heading with the actual attributes of a particular person in that category. Thus in turn were considered physical capacities, intelligence, special aptitudes, knowledge in terms of general educational level required and specific skills, disposition, aims and interests, and opportunities and circumstances. The second method of job analysis is a simple extension of this scheme in job analysis form.

Job Analysis: Method 2

1. JOB TITLE.
2. SEX. Is job restricted to either males or to females?
3. AGE RANGE. Are there any statutory requirements? In addition preferences should be given.
4. PHYSICAL REQUIREMENTS. Most jobs have certain physical requirements or bars. In some height, colour vision, hearing, etc., are specifically emphasized. Equally as important are factors in the job which require the person doing it to have endurance, strength, sense of smell, etc. These may not be statutory but are important job factors.
5. ATTAINMENTS:
   (a) *General.* The educational level required; e.g. school certificate, university entrance standard, etc. Any particular subjects which seem to be of help in the job. The general educational level as a social factor must also be taken into account.
   (b) *Technical.* Are there any professional or trade certificates which must be held? This includes degrees, diplomas, and intern or apprenticeship certificates.

6. ABILITY:

(a) *General intelligence.* The general level of intelligence required for a job can be an excellent guide to an employee's suitability. It must be remembered that too much intelligence is often as bad as, if not worse than, too little.

(b) *Specific aptitudes.* Many jobs require particular, specific aptitudes for their successful completion. An applicant for a clerical job, for example, must have a gift for spotting errors, filing things correctly, checking, etc. This is something distinct from acquired knowledge and depends not merely on training. Some people have a gift in handling particular sorts of materials, others have not. The common aptitudes which should be considered for each job are:

Clerical	Artistic/Musical
Mechanical	Arithmetical/Mathematical
Verbal expression, etc.	

7. INTERESTS. Interests seem to be linked with success in a job in two ways. Firstly, a particular interest may be involved in a job itself. For example, an interest in repairing or constructing things would match with a repair or construction job. Often a particular job demands of the person doing it a particular set of interests. The field of social work, for example, demands interest in being with other people, helping, persuading, understanding, and teaching them. A research worker must be interested in sifting evidence and solving logical problems.

The second way in which interests must be considered relates to general interests not specifically connected with the job. Often people who carry out a particular job seem time and again to appear with certain interests seemingly unconnected with the job. In this sense, interests emerge as factors which either indicate the general degree of energy required by the job or the sort of person who fits into the job, or they indicate common ways of filling needs not met by the job itself. In any case they are important factors for analysis.

8. PERSONALITY REQUIREMENTS. Personality is a term used in a number of ways both technically and in popular speech. Psychologically it refers to the essential characteristics of a person as they distinguish that person from all others. One can think of an individual's personality as the amalgam of all his impulses and ideals, opinions, beliefs, and sentiments. It identifies his customary and habitual way of looking at life and his customary and habitual ways of acting or behaving. The personality requirements of a job can also be assessed in many ways. Probably the simplest method is first to give a general pen-picture of the sort of person who succeeds in the job and then to itemize any specific personality traits which might be required. A list of personality traits or qualities is given in Table 2.1 as a guide to be used when considering what is required in any particular situation. In making the analysis, always remember that there may be some personalities which would not fit into the job, and therefore some traits may need to be mentioned as being ones which would exclude from the job anyone who possessed them.

9. SATISFACTIONS AND PROBLEMS:
   (a) A statement of the various satisfactions the job offers. This includes the promotion prospects, the present status, the measure of security, or alternately variety and adventure which the job offers.
   (b) The reverse side of the picture must also be given showing the limitations of the job — the factors which are liable to frustrate or annoy those individuals who have not got the correct personality and tolerance to accept them. If any reasons for previous failure in the job are known, these should be given here.

10. SOCIAL AND GENERAL:
    (a) Human beings are not merely individuals they are also social beings. Hence it is necessary to consider the social background of the person and the social setting of the job. Will the individual be satisfied with the

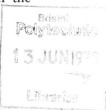

TABLE 2.1 *List of personality traits for use with
job analysis. Method 2*

Aggressive	Good-natured
Attentive to people	Grasping
Adaptable	
Assertive	Hard
Adventurous	Happy-go-lucky
Aloof	Hypochondriacal
Artistic	
Ambitious	Initiative
Anxious	Independent-minded
Attention getting	Incommunicative
	Imaginative
Boorish	Irritable
Brooding	Insightful regarding self
	Insightful regarding others
Calm	
Co-operative	Jealous
Conventional	
Cheerful	Kindly
Conscientious	
Carefree	Low morale
Considerate .	Lacking frustration tolerance
Critical of others	Languid
	Lacking self-insight
Dependable	
Dependent on others	Morbid
Depressed	Moody
Determined	
Demanding	Neurotic
	Nervous
Emotionally mature	Narrow interests
Evasive	
Easy going	Obstructive
Emotional	Outgoing
Esthetic	Orderly
Expedient ("cuts corners")	
Exacting and fussy	Persevering
	Phlegmatic
Frivolous	Practical
Frank and open	Permissive
Fickle	Polished and socially alert
Friendly	
Fastidious	

Quick thinking	Shy
	Suspicious
Realistic	Sound judgement
Responsible	Socially alert
Relaxed	Sensitive
Responsive and genial	
Retiring	Trustful
Restrained	Tolerant
Resilient	Tough
	Talkative
Self-disciplined	
Self-sufficient	Unconventional
Severe	
Solemn	Worrying
Self-assured	Withdrawn
Submissive	Warm and gregarious
Smug	

working conditions of the job? Will his family fit in and adjust to the way of life the job carries with it? A particular occupation may demand long hours or shift work which could well upset the employee's family and through them the employee himself. In a different family the wife might be irked by a husband whose hours of work were short, he being always under her feet.

(b) Leading on from a consideration of the pressures of the social factors involved in a job, one must finally consider the various relationships of different parts of the analysis. Although we have discussed personality and intellectual requirements as two separate issues; it may be that the relationship of one to the other is significant. For example, the absence of a preferred personality trait may well not matter in an individual whose ability is high although it would be more important in a candidate whose aptitude was low. The relationship of attitudes to needs, and both these to the satisfactions the job offers, frequently produces additional information which is entered here.

Job Analysis: Method 3

1. JOB TITLE.
2. DUTIES. Both a general description and a detailed breakdown are given of the duties involved, identifying the nature of the work: the following sub-headings are suggested for the detailed analysis:

   (a) *Skills involved* — technical, manual, organizational, and judgmental.
   (b) *Effort required* — physical and mental demands made on the individual.
   (c) *Responsibilities* — both for material or equipment and for the work safety of others.

3. JOB CONDITIONS. A statement is given of the physical working conditions, the physical environment in which the job is performed. Special mention is made of any particular hazards or adverse conditions which exist.
4. QUALIFICATIONS REQUIRED:
   (a) *Sex* — is the job restricted to either males or females?
   (b) *Age* — is there a minimum or maximum age for entry?
   (c) *Physical requirements* — are there any medical requirements or bars? What physical capacities are required?
   (d) *Attainments:*
      (i) General education — school level, certificates or diplomas required. Is higher education an essential?
     (ii) Technical education — the specialist training required of an entrant, either on-the-job or through part or full-time further education
    (iii) Experience — some attainments are gained through experience; is previous experience in a junior position or related job required?
   (e) *Abilities:*
      (i) General intelligence — what level of intelligence must the person have to cope with this job? Is there an upper limit?
     (ii) Special aptitudes — are there any special aptitudes

related to success in the job, which it is advisable for the person concerned to possess?

(f) *Interests* — which occupational interest area is related to this job?

(g) *Personality requirements* — which personality traits or characteristics enable a person to fit into this occupational area and cope with the problems and human factors inherent in the job?

(h) *Social requirements* — does the job require a particular life style or set patterns of social behaviour (e.g. minister of religion)?

5. POSITION AND PROSPECTS

Through a number of subheadings, this section surveys the career prospects in the occupation being studied:

(a) *Employment opportunities* — are there regular job vacancies locally or on the national level?

(b) *Entry* — how do you go about obtaining your first position?

(c) *Salary or wages* — what are the average earnings at entry and at later times? Is there a scale? Does experience count? Do qualifications count?

(d) *Promotion* — are there channels for promotion? If so, what is regarded as the normal career grade? How many in the occupation rise higher to senior positions?

(e) *Satisfactions and problems* — what are the satisfactions offered through work in this job and what frustrations and limitations are there?

Isolating the Critical Requirements

We saw in the first chapter that if you ask the interview to do too much it then loses reliability. Although you now have a comprehensive job analysis, this in itself is not sufficient. It is just not possible for anyone to cope with all these factors in one interview. Furthermore, the interview is not even a suitable or appropriate measuring instrument for many of the factors.

When, for example, you are concerned with assessing technical efficiency at some skill or trade, then, as Vernon and Parry, and Kelly and Fiske have shown, a good standardized test will provide you with better, more reliable, and valid information. Therefore, on both these grounds it is necessary at this stage to isolate from the job analysis a few relevant factors which are the important factors for selection. These should be relevant in the sense that they are accessible to assessment in the interview and that they form the critical requirements for selection.

It is virtually impossible to give a rule-of-thumb procedure for isolating the critical requirements. All one can do is to offer one or two guiding principles. Firstly, it would seem from experience that there should be not more than half a dozen of these critical requirements at the most. The interviewer – who is after all only a human being – can cope with up to six factors with little difficulty. To ask him to assess more, however, is asking too much of him and his interview, so that any gain in quantity of assessment will be more than negated by a drop in quality. In deciding what these four, five, or six requirements should be, your best plan is to work through the job analysis considering each point mentioned in it against the question: This is a preferable thing but is it essential? For any point to be accepted as a critical requirement you must be satisfied that it is an essential characteristic of the person, a characteristic which will make the difference between that person's success or failure on the job. Since these critical requirements are to be the factors on which assessment and prediction will be based, it is essential that you obtain the correct ones. In fact, being based on subjective judgements all along, you can never be 100% sure they are correct. You can, however, ensure that they are not far from correct by taking not only your opinion but a combined decision of what they are, taken from a number of people. The best way of producing the critical requirements is to gather together three or four or more people, all of whom have a good knowledge of the job in question and if possible of related jobs and of the industry or organization where the job exists. This group then works through the analysis and discusses each point in turn so that the eventually agreed critical requirements will be the product of a team decision. There will, of course, be many instances where such an approach is just not possible. In this event you can still be assured of producing reasonably valid critical requirements provided that they emerge from a systematic point-by-point appraisal of the job analysis.

As the final check on the adequacy of the list of critical requirements you have produced, it is useful to check them against a set of criteria which define a "critical requirement". A set of criteria for use in this way is shown in Table 2.2.

TABLE 2.2. *Criteria for acceptance as a critical requirement*

---

1. To form an acceptable critical requirement for an assessment interview a factor must:
   (a) Be critical to successful performances in the job in question.
   (b) Be a human characteristic which is assessable through the interview.
2. Criteria for acceptability:
   (a) Definitions of critical requirements must be couched in terms which are both *precise* and *communicable.*
   (b) Critical requirements must differentiate people on an occupational basis (i.e. a factor cannot be used as a useful critical requirement if all workers, all applicants possess it).
   (c) The dimension must be relevant to satisfactory performance in the job in question; *or*
   It must be a stipulated entry requirement.
   (d) The dimension must be one which persists in the individual over time.
   (e) Critical requirements for the interview must fall within the range of characteristics appropriate to assessment by that method.

Establishing Critical Requirements — An Example

The second method of job analysis forms the basis for this example which shows how the critical requirements for a selection assessment interview are isolated in practice. The job is that of a reservations telephone clerk in New Zealand National Airways Corporation, employed at one of the city branches of the Corporation. The reservations section of the branch is situated in a light airy room on the second floor of the building. Reservations are made on a card system which is housed in two long, troughed tables. Printed cards are filed, one for each flight, each day. Cards are filed in the troughs in chronological order and according to date, cards being available for approximately three-month periods. A further classification is made in that cards for northbound flights are housed in the right-hand side table and those for southbound flights in the left-hand table. A centre block in each table holds a simpler system of cards for recording applications for return bookings, whilst on the end of the left-hand table a block contains cards for outward Sunday flights both northbound and southbound. The reservations clerks operate between the two tables. Each clerk has a plug-in phone and there are four multi-line phone turrets on each table. This enables the clerk to move around and use the nearest phone without losing contact with the customer and without the whole section being hindered by long, trailing phone leads. The clerks deal with applications for bookings from three sources. Firstly, requests for seats come from the public counter of the branch downstairs where counter clerks pass on customers' requests. Secondly, local agents, travel bureaux, etc., request tickets. Finally, the general public rings through directly for seats.

Simply outlined the job is as follows: the clerk, who can be male or female, answers a call as soon as possible after a turret light indicates someone is ringing in. Referring to the clerk as "he" for simplicity, his first task is to find out what is required. If the call comes from the branch counter or from an agent, this is usually simple since difficulties and alternatives which the passenger has in mind will already have been dealt with. In the case of a direct call, the clerk may be faced with a query of the variety which sounds something like this: — "Can you book me to A via B on Tuesday, or is it Wednesday, anyway it's the fourth?" If asked what time of the day, the answer will probably be: "Oh, morning I suppose, though not too late, or I could go late evening providing we got in before dark." Dealing with such problems occupies about 12% of the time of the clerk, and whilst talking to the customer or agent on the phone he will probably be checking cards at the same time to find available flights, alternatives, and possible seats. Once a definite request for a booking is made on a specific flight on a specific day, the booking must be entered on the appropriate card. This is done by entering the passenger's name on the card together with address and, if possible, telephone number for contacting. When complete the entry is checked with the passenger, the day, date, flight number, and time being reported back to them. In addition to these, certain additional duties are entailed which are generally of a checking and passenger-contact variety. Since this analysis was made, computerized booking has been introduced. However, the job remains basically the same save in its clerical components and that the checking of reservations and seat availability is now carried out on-line to the computer.

Three independent analyses were made — one by myself after a period of observation and discussions with the section supervisor, one by a member of the personnel branch, and the third by a group of administration officers of the Corporation. The results of the three were pooled, after discussions, into the final form which is given below.

1. JOB TITLE. Reservations Clerk (Large Branch) N.A.C. on telephone bookings. (Note that the title is given with precision to distinguish this job from a general small centre clerk and from a counter clerk.)
2. SEX. Male or female.
3. AGE. Normally minimum age of 17, but someone of 16 with suitable educational qualifications could be accepted. In practice this is rarely done. The maximum age for first appointment is 25. The preferable age is a "mature 20" and few are taken on less than 19. (Not only is the Head Office statutory regulation regarding minimum age quoted, but also what happens in practice. This is so here, and will often be different.)
4. PHYSICAL REQUIREMENTS. Good eyesight in order to read cards with small print and handwriting. Good hearing

since most of the work is done through phones. Reasonably active and of good stamina since job requires the clerk to stand all day, move about frequently, and reach over wide tables. For continued Corporation service a good physical appearance is required since promotion is by way of jobs which require contact with the public.

5. ATTAINMENTS:
   (a) A minimum of three years' secondary education preferably with a School Certificate.
   (b) Writing must be legible. A reasonable knowledge of New Zealand geographical locations and sound written English are both additional advantages.

6. ABILITY:
   (a) *General intelligence.* No validated test results, but general opinion was that clerks should not be less than average. Ability to think quickly and to remain mentally alert was also deemed essential.
   (b) *Special aptitudes.* Clerical and arithmetical aptitudes are essential.

7. INTERESTS. The clerk should be interested in people and have a liking for dealing with the public. This should apply particularly to helping people with their travel problems. An interest in travel and also in aviation would be of advantage but of lesser importance than the basic interests.

8. PERSONALITY REQUIREMENTS. The clerk should be bright, cheerful, tactful, and well-mannered and able to retain these attributes when working under pressure. He should be willing to keep on learning and amenable to change. Important personality traits are: patience, adaptability, tolerance, willingness to co-operate. He should have a reasonable command of spoken English though this is regarded not as a requirement in itself but as a sign of a good public manner. In essence the successful clerk has what might be called a good public relations manner and attitude so that he leaves with the prospective passenger a generally pleasant impression of his first contact with the Corporation.

9. SATISFACTIONS AND PROBLEMS. Most clerks find satisfaction in serving the public and in getting away from a desk job to one in an expanding organization which offers a wide variety of problems. Those seeking opportunity for travel and good promotion prospects can find both here. Poor manners on the phone, and an inability to deal with customers' problems constitute a problem to some workers. In a predominantly 9 to 5 country, this job operates on shift work which therefore poses a major problem to adjustment in young people.

10. SOCIAL AND GENERAL:

(a) Of central importance in terms of public acceptance in this job is a good social manner. A pleasant speaking voice of reasonably "cultured" tones is essential. At the same time, acceptability to colleagues indicates that the clerk must not "put on airs and graces". For promotion, neat dress habits are essential.

(b) The job is at times monotonous when no calls are coming in; at other times activity is fast and furious, calling for a grasp of a wide variety of instructions, time-tables, fares, and facilities: the ability to tolerate both at periods is essential. Since shift work is required, outside interests must be of a sort to fit. A regular Saturday afternoon footballer who "lives for the game" might find it difficult to adjust.

The group of Administration Officers, two members of Head Office Personnel Staff, and myself then proceeded to isolate from the general analysis the critical requirements which would be assessed in the interview. These critical requirements, it should be noted, relate only to the interview. Other factors, such as clerical or arithmetical aptitude, may also be critical, but it would not be appropriate to attempt to assess them from an interview.

The interview critical requirements were isolated by going through each of the headings in the analysis and as a group discussing the various points contained there. The discussions were aimed at picking out the points most agreed upon as being of central importance. When the group was in doubt, we asked ourselves the question: Without this factor or requirement, can people succeed in the job? In this way the analysis was reduced for our purposes to the following five critical requirements:

(1) Pleasant appearance and manner
(2) Interest in people, particularly in terms of a "service" job.
(3) Adaptable yet patient of frustration.
(4) Willingness to accept shift work.
(5) Career attitude — looking to future in Corporation rather than here and now.

When candidates were interviewed, using the techniques outlined in the following chapter, the interviewer now had a specific assessment task. The interviewer's job was now not merely to "sum up" this candidate but to rate him on these five specific and known points. In this way the task of the interview has been restricted to one within its powers and the possibility for bias or personal prejudice reduced.

CHAPTER 3

The "DOs" and "DON'Ts" of Interviewing

This chapter is concerned with the actual conduct of the interview itself. We have seen in the previous chapter how we can produce for each interview a specific task. How four or five critical factors can be isolated, factors which we must look for in the candidate, factors which we must rate the candidate on, since success in the job has been shown to depend on the possession of them to an adequate degree. These critical requirements limit the purview of the interview, restricting the area of assessment. This makes the interviewer's task easier, on the one hand, and, on the other, lessens bias and increases reliability. To limit the scope of the interview alone, however, is obviously not sufficient to ensure its being reliable or to ensure that it produces an unbiased, unprejudiced, and valid assessment. To achieve such a satisfactory assessment through an interview requires the controlling of three basic areas. These can be summarized as follows:

(1) The background, initial work in organizing and planning the interview, and the interview programme.
(2) The orientation and attitude of mind which the interviewer has both to the interview and to the candidate who has to be assessed.
(3) The method of conducting the interview which the interviewer has, his manner with the candidate, and his ways of obtaining information.

The first of these has for its main part been dealt with in the previous chapter. The essentially important thing in the organization of an interview programme for selection is that the interviewer should know exactly what it is he has to assess, and this he will know if the critical requirements have previously been isolated. The question of organization does include also the planning, timing, receiving of candidates, the preparation of rooms, and the completing of necessary paper work — the many administrative details which are so easily forgotten. Easily forgotten or not, they remain important points and so will be treated in slightly more detail in a later chapter.

It is with the second two points that we are concerned in this chapter since they determine what the interviewer does in his attempts at assessment. The second point concerns the attitudes of the interviewer, and these in one sense at least will control the third point since, according to the attitudes to the situation the interviewer has, so will he behave. If the interviewer starts the interview with the attitude that he is going to meet a crafty, lying, scheming individual who will sell himself without reference to the truth, then the interviewer's behaviour is liable to be antagonistic if not hostile towards the candidate. I remember a P.S.O. in one of the services whose attitude was that unless you could surprise the interviewee and get under his guard you would not be told the truth. Working on this conviction, therefore, he literally barricaded himself in by piling books, boxes, and assorted whatnots about his desk. From behind this shelter he would pop up at intervals and throw out questions of shattering intent to his surprised opponent. Whilst illustrating how not to interview, this also shows clearly how the interviewer's behaviour and interviewing method is linked closely to his attitude towards the interview.

What is required is a plan or guide which, while retaining the flexibility and open nature of the interview which is one of its main strengths, will at the same time control the attitudes of the interviewer and his behaviour during the interview. For such a method we are indebted almost entirely to one set of research workers — those engaged in the Hawthorne Works studies at the Western Electric Company. As a result of earlier experimental studies which have now become *the* nursery primer for all industrial psychologists, the Western Electric Company decided to embark on an interview project, one of the aims of which was to assess employee complaints, their causes, and relations to work output. From these small beginnings grew a new concept of interviewing as can be seen in the detailed report on the Hawthorne studies written by Roethlisberger and Dickson (1950) on which the following is based.

The Hawthorne interviewers began by using the then standard interview technique of having a set questionnaire. This does ensure standardization of the interview but, as I pointed out earlier, it is the flexibility of the interview which is its strong point, and a set list of questions to be asked of each and every candidate allows for little flexibility. Furthermore, the Hawthorne interviewers found that it was very difficult to ask the questions in such a way that they did not in themselves suggest a special significance or particular answer to the interviewee. It was, in fact, difficult for the interviewer not to bias the result by the manner in which he asked the question. At the same time, the interviewer had to take an active part in the interview; he had to take the controlling role and guide the interview in the right direction. In terms of the present analysis in this book, he had to keep the discussion on points which would throw light on the critical requirements. What was required was some scheme which would do two things: keep the interviewer's attitudes free and unbiased and yet allow him to guide the interview correctly. This need was met by the Hawthorne workers in two sets of rules: rules for orientation of the interviewer and rules for the conduct of the interview.

Rules of Orientation

The Hawthorne rules of orientation attempt to show the interviewer what the correct attitude should be towards the interview and the candidate (Table 3.1). They suggest the frame of mind in which the interviewer should enter upon his task.

Since they are dealing with the mental or emotional attitudes of the interviewer and are concerned with how he is going to interpret what emerges in the interview, they cannot be explicit instructions simply followed. They are more in the nature of "mood music" aimed at producing the correct feeling in the interviewer for what follows.

TABLE 3.1 *The Hawthorne rules of orientation for interviewing*

(This table is extracted from page 272 of *Management and the worker* by F. J. Roethlisberger and W. J. Dickson, published by Harvard University Press)

Rule I.   The interviewer should treat what is said in an interview as an item in a context.
  (a) The interviewer should not pay exclusive attention to the manifest content of the intercourse.
  (b) The interviewer should not treat everything that is said as either fact or error.
  (c) The interviewer should not treat everything that is said as being at the same psychological level.

Rule II.   The interviewer should listen not only to what a person wants to say but also for what he does not want to say or cannot say without help.

Rule III. The interviewer should treat the mental contexts described in the preceding rules as indices and seek through them the personal reference that is being revealed.

Rule IV. The interviewer should keep the personal reference in its social context.
  (a) The interviewer should remember that the interview is itself a social situation, and that therefore the social relation existing between the interviewer and the interviewee is in part determining what is said.
  (b) The interviewer should see to it that the speaker's sentiments do not act on his own.

Rule I warns the interviewer that in his assessment of what is said in the interview he must be sophisticated. The things a candidate says are all part of an interview, an interview on the results of which his future career may depend. Thus what he says must take into account that he is involved in the interview situation. This is stressed more fully in Rule IV(a), where the fact that the interview itself can bias the assessment, is put into different words. Returning to Rule I, however, this goes even further. It warns that anything a person says must be judged not as a statement in isolation but as a remark made in a certain situation by a particular individual, with his own unique constellation of experiences and responsiveness. This suggests that it is extremely important for the interviewer to know the background of the candidates he is interviewing. The Scottish schoolboy who tells you he has a paper round is merely showing that he is following the Scottish tradition and being a lad of parts — or perhaps more wildly, following wistfully in the footsteps of Andrew Carnegie. The London schoolboy with the paper round may well have very different reasons.

Rule I(b) and (c) take this warning even further. Not everything is black or white, nor is everything at the same psychological level. The fisherman who says the one that got away was 2 foot long when in reality it was a mere 6 inches is not a perjurer condemned to eternal damnation, nor is the girl who tells you she hates coffee to be judged equal to the racist, black or white, who tells you he hates all foreigners. The examples may be trivial, but the lesson is, I think, clear.

In the second rule the emphasis is on the interviewer as a critical listener. The rule suggests that in his approach to the interview the interviewer should constantly be on the lookout for gaps and omissions in what is said. It does two further things, too, of fundamental importance to interviewing. It sets the scene for the interviewer to take a listening role and also to be a helper in its suggestion that some of your assessment information will only come if you can help the candidate to produce it. This suggests a much more subtle approach and role for the interviewer than that of the mere questioner. This same emphasis emerges in Rule III, where it is suggested that it is not so much the actual things which are said, not the facts which emerge, but the light these things throw upon the character, personality, or general make-up of the candidate concerned, and, of course, the evidence they give you about the critical requirements. The interviewer does not set out to obtain facts about certain events but attempts to get the candidate talking about himself and judges from this conversation what sort of person he has in front of him, particularly as regards those aspects which are involved in the critical requirements.

Rules for Conducting the Interview

In contrast to the "mood music" nature of the orientation rules, these rules for the conduct of the interview are the specific instructions — how to behave in the interview itself (Table 3.2). These are the rules which tell you what you should and should not do. They are straightforward and largely self-explanatory — although experience suggests that they are easier to understand than to obey.

TABLE 3.2. *The Hawthorne rules for
conducting the interview*
(This table is extracted from page 287 of *Management
and the Worker* by F. J. Roethlisberger and W. J. Dickson,
published by Harvard University Press)

Rule I.   The interviewer should listen to the speaker in a patient and friendly but intelligently critical manner.
Rule II.   The interviewer should not display any kind of authority.
Rule III. The interviewer should not give advice or moral admonition.
Rule IV.   The interviewer should not argue with the speaker.
Rule V.   The interviewer should talk or ask questions only under certain conditions:
        (a) To help the person talk.
        (b) To relieve any fears or anxieties on the part of the speaker which may be affecting his relation to the interviewer.
        (c) To praise the interviewee for reporting his thoughts and feelings accurately.
        (d) To veer the discussion to some topic which has been omitted or neglected.
        (e) To discuss implicit assumptions if this is advisable.

A new vista of interviewing is opened up where instead of factual questions and answers the main aim of the interview is to get the candidate talking about himself. Of course, there must be some restriction to the range of conversation, and Rule V(d) implies that there is a particular set of topics which you want discussed. These are, for our purposes, those topics bearing on the critical requirements.

A Framework for the Interview

The picture of the kind of interview we should aim at producing begins to emerge. It is not a stilted affair of set questions, which are not varied from one applicant to another. Rather it is a live, active, two-way conversation in which the interviewee is encouraged to play the major role. The tone of this interaction process is set by the interviewer through the orientation he has to interviewing and his consequent conduct in the interview. The direction the interaction takes should be guided by the interviewer to throw light on the special purpose of the interview — the assessment of a set of critical requirements. Although he does not use a set list of questions, the interviewer does need some plan for action which will enable him to guide the conversation on to relevant and significant topics. To put the Hawthorne rules into useful practice I feel one cannot do better than to ally them to what has been called the biographical approach to interviewing. The biographical approach sets out in the interview to obtain a picture of the life history of the candidate. The interviewer using this method will try to find out from the candidate what he has done, what he thinks about what he has done, his interests and hobbies, both as they are now and as they have been, his relationship to friends, school and working colleagues, and family; in short, through talking about the candidate's likes, dislikes, fears and hopes, past activities and future plans, he should arrive at a reasonably clear conception of the kind of person the interviewee is.

In fact, we are not essentially interested in all the behaviour patterns but only certain relevant ones. The biography can be restricted to one or two areas only and in so doing will make the interviewer's task easier and the prospects better for a reliable and valid assessment. This restriction of interest can be achieved by having the candidate fill in a pre-interview form which will cover those details about the candidate's past history which are relevant to the critical requirements. In following Rule V(a) the interviewer can refer to the form and get the candidate talking about matters which are mentioned there. The form also helps to veer discussions in the correct directions and is a constant guide to the topics which have to be covered. What I have said here implies that no one form will cover all situations, and this is the case. Changing the form according to the situation helps to retain flexibility and also ensures that the specific task for each assessment situation is carried into the interview itself. Varying the form also allows one to concentrate on relevant factors for the general category of people being interviewed. For younger interviewees, for example, emphasis is placed on school and parental home circumstances. For the older interviewee, emphasis may be better placed on factors like employment history and the individual's own interpersonal and social life. Thus it is best to plan a specific form for your own use in the situations in which you are called upon to interview. Most application forms or pre-interview questionnaires, however, are variations on a theme. Keeping in mind the limited range of assessment areas relevant to assessment through the interview, this is hardly surprising. The five major biographical—personal data areas outlined in Table 3.3 are in fact the areas on which most pre-interview blanks are based. By selecting appropriate areas then organizing a questionnaire about these areas, the interviewer can construct a form for his own purposes.

Table 3.4 provides an excellent example of a specific form developed for use with one large, general group of interviewees, the 15+-year-old adolescent. It was developed at the Applied Psychology Unit of the University of Edinburgh and is based on an original to be found in Sir Cyril Burt's *The Young Delinquent* (1925).

The form places emphasis on school and associated activities in which an adolescent might well be expected to be engaged. The section dealing with employment, on the other hand, is limited and is mainly concerned with finding out whether the youngster has had part-time jobs at school and what he has done since leaving, if indeed he has left school. It makes no attempt to find details of his jobs which a form intended for adults might well do. None the less, in the present version the section concerned with employment is sufficient to enable the interviewer, through it, to veer the conversation to discuss the candidate's attitudes, and possibly his parents' views, on part-time work and choice of career; this, of course, is all that it is intended to do. One final point is worth noting. The form is not comprehensive nor does the information asked for give any details of the various pursuits. This is deliberate, since the intent of the form is merely to provide stimuli to conversation in the interview. If it were possible to obtain the fully detailed account you require from the form, then the form alone would be a sufficient selection tool without an interview.

TABLE 3.3 *Possible biographical aspects to be included on the application blank*

A. *Personal circumstances.* Candidate's age, physical health, marital and family status, normal place of residence, mobility, etc.
B. *Educational record.* Primary, secondary, and tertiary education, further education (full or part-time), on-the-job training, apprenticeships, attainment certificates, degrees or diplomas achieved, and skills mastered.
C. *Occupational record.* Number and nature of jobs, reasons for leaving, promotions offered and accepted, satisfaction with and satisfactoriness of occupational history.
D. *Interests and activities.* His occupational, educational, and socially related interests, his cultural and sporting activities, and spare time hobbies.
E. *Personal aspirations.* Career aims, personal aims, ambitions, salary and/or other status expectations.

This brings us back to the whole question of the relevance of the interview. If we want to establish factual matters of certificates, history, attainments, etc., then the interview is not the method to use. If one of your critical requirements is an above-average ability in mathematics or a high degree of mechanical aptitude, then the more efficient way of assessing these factors would be to use standardized tests. It is when you are concerned with less-tangible aspects of the candidate's personality, his interest patterns, his attitudes, his character and temperament, that the interview emerges as the appropriate assessment tool. For the interview shows the candidate not as an assemblage of written data, not through his answers to certain technical questions, but as a real, live, "going" person, talking about himself and his way of life. It presents not a static list of accomplishments but a dynamic and living picture of a human being.

The Interviewer's Basic Skills and Techniques

It is the interviewer's job to obtain this living picture of the candidate, particularly in terms of certain critical aspects. In carrying out this task the interviewer uses the pre-interview form as a starting-out point (Table 3.4), but it is his own skill as

TABLE 3.4. *An example of an interview form which may be amended for various purposes*

Full name: .... Date of birth: ....

Name of school	Dates attended From To	Highest class reached
(i)		
(ii)		
(iii)		

Best (or favourite) subjects: ....

....

Worst (or disliked) subjects: ....

....

Games: ....

Clubs, Societies, Cadets, etc.: ....

....

Underline any of the following activities in which you have taken part, or in which you are actively interested:

WOODWORK   CYCLE REPAIRS   ELECTRICAL RADIO REPAIRS

METALWORK   MOTOR REPAIRS   MUSIC

PHOTOGRAPHY   CYCLING   WATCH OR CLOCK REPAIRS

DRAWING   BUILDING KITS   STAMP COLLECTING

CAMPING   BOATING   HOUSECRAFT

FISHING   READING   Any others: ....

DEBATING   DRAMATICS   ....

COOKERY   NEEDLEWORK   ....

Employment (including part-time jobs):

	Firm	Your job	Wages
(i)			
(ii)			
(iii)			

Date: ....   Signature: ....

an interviewer on which the value of the assessment depends. This skill, which is defined in the role of the interviewer, is best seen as the carrying through of the Hawthorne rules for interviewing, for these in turn define the actual role of the interviewer.

The first and primary skill is that of listening. This is not merely a listening with the ear but with the whole body. Ivey (1971) refers to this most basic of the interviewer's skills as "attending". You show your interest and attention by looking at the interviewee, by sitting alertly, and by responding with the odd word or phrase to show you have been listening. Contrast this approach with that of the interviewer who slouches in his chair, seems taken up with some correspondence on the desk, makes surreptitious glances at his wrist watch, and when he has run out of other things to do gazes steadfastly at some point above the interviewee's head. Obviously he is not *really* listening and so the interviewee does not bother to tell him anything. It is, in fact, surprising on how few occasions when we are in "conversation" that we really listen to the other fellow. Most of the time we are more likely to be waiting for a gap to occur in the "noise" being emitted by that other guy so that we can get in our say. One effective way of improving listening skills is to use the human relations training game "listening triads". Three participants are required – A and B as communicators and C as observer and assessor. A and B are allocated or select a topic for discussion. A begins and has about 2 minutes to give his first contribution to the discussion. He then hands over to B, who before contributing his own thoughts has to summarize in 30 seconds what A has said. He then may introduce fresh ideas of his own for the next 2 minutes. The discussion is continued for about 15 to 20 minutes, and at each changeover the next speaker must begin by summarizing what has gone before. Participant C acts as timekeeper and also assesses the adequacy of the summaries the contributors make, providing feedback on the effectiveness of the two contributors. Using this technique forces A and B to truly "listen" and attend to each other; unless they do they do not get a chance to contribute to the interaction themselves.

Listening encourages the interviewee to talk, and the aim of the interview is to get the interviewee to talk spontaneously about the relevant personal data areas for the interview's purpose. The interviewer's role is to say as little as possible but to encourage the interviewee to talk. To do this the interviewer begins by inviting the interviewee to talk about himself or by asking open-ended questions about a significant area. Questions should be phrased in such a way that "yes" and "no" are not possible or likely answers. Whenever possible the interviewee should be encouraged to reveal his thoughts and feelings. This can readily be achieved by phrasing questions in an appropriate form: What are your feelings about working with ....? The interviewer can then effectively follow up by *paraphrasing* the interviewee's response. Paraphrasing is a useful technique, indicating understanding and interest and often encouraging the interviewee to talk further. In a similar way, summarizing, as practised in the listening triads game, can also be useful. It allows the interviewee the opportunity to correct any misinterpretations, and if adequately done shows that the interviewer has been attending. It also gives an opportunity for the interviewee to talk further about any issue he feels has not been sufficiently emphasized. The interviewer can encourage this by such questions as: How do you see the important issues in that? or Which of these experiences did *you* find most important? In testing the range of attitudes or feelings in this way, it is important not to forget negative aspects. The interviewer may, for example, get the interviewee to talk about a job he has had, saying: "Tell me about this job you had as ...." If the interviewee expresses liking for the job, the interviewer may wish to comment: "You've told me how much you liked the job, was there anything you *disliked* about it?"

Interviewees will vary in their responsiveness, and not all will be ready talkers. Some will be monosyllabic and the interviewer will find himself talking more than he wishes. He should beware of the temptation to jump in, conversationally speaking, as soon as there is silence for a moment. Providing he remains attentive and the overall atmosphere is relaxed, the occasional moment's silence may be a useful part of the whole interaction situation, encouraging the interviewee to further conversation.

Putting it all together we have a new concept of interviewing. In this approach the interviewer is no longer seen as an inquisitor but rather as a friendly person helping the interviewee to talk about himself. By his relaxed, yet attentive manner, the interviewer sets the scene. Then the interview proceeds along the lines indicated by the Hawthorne rules, which can be summarized in terms of the following four basic requirements for good interviewing.

(1) Get the interviewee to talk — and then let him talk.
(2) Above all else, listen, but listen intelligently and critically.
(3) Lead the talk on to particular topics as specified by the critical requirements.
(4) Interpret what is said as throwing light on the interviewee's nature or personality.

CHAPTER 4

A Case Study in Interviewing

In the previous chapters I have put forward a method of interviewing aimed at controlling bias and prejudice and increasing reliability and validity. Within the confines of a book it is difficult to add to the formal statement of the method any practical experience of it. The only possible way of showing how the system works in practice seems to be through the use of a case study. The following one is therefore presented so that you can see something of interviewing in a practical situation. Practice can be compared with the formal statement of the two preceding chapters and the reader can judge for himself its effectiveness. Few interviews in real life are perfect; neither is this case study interview. In fact at least two deliberate but minor faults are introduced to provide a basis for discussion. No doubt any critical reader will find many more mistakes and omissions which, far from being deliberate, are unobserved errors, reflecting my own weaknesses in interview technique.

A final warning, which refers to all case studies and not merely this one, must be given. Although based on fact, this is not the report of an actual example. It is hypothetical and representative, written as an illustration rather than being an extract from any specific interview programme. On the one hand, this has the advantage that the case study can simplify and highlight the important points. On the other hand, its artificiality still prevents the true nature of the interview being fully revealed.

The Critical Requirements

The case study concerns the interview assessment of a candidate during a selection programme for airline pilots. The first step concerns the isolation of the critical requirements which are to be looked for in the interview. These, of course, are isolated in turn from the general job analysis. This is presented here, using the second method of analysis shown in Chapter 2.

1. JOB TITLE. Short-haul airline pilot (National Corporation).

2. SEX. Male.

3. AGE RANGE. 21–28 on entry. Because of promotion, which is based on age, applicants should by preference be not older than 24 or 25 years of age.

4. PHYSICAL REQUIREMENTS. Must be A1 physically, perfect vision (with or without glasses), hearing acute, lungs and heart satisfactory, and no permanent sinus trouble.

5. ATTAINMENTS:
   (a) *General.* A sound general education is essential. Normally a General Certificate in Education or School Certificate is required as a prerequisite, but in exceptional circumstances this may be waived.
   (b) *Technical.* Must have a Private Pilot's Licence and sufficient flying hours to be near qualification for a Commercial Pilot's Licence. The possession of a C.P.L. is a distinct advantage. Experience in multi-engined aircraft is also an advantage. The trainee should possess sufficient technical knowledge to be able to cope with training courses on aircraft systems — mechanical, electrical, etc.

6. ABILITY:
   (a) *General intelligence.* No set test results are available, but a study of the training course suggests that the level should not be less than high average.

(b) *Specific aptitudes*. (i) Flying. (ii) Mechanical: general ability to think and solve problems in "mechanical" terms. (iii) Reasonable arithmetical/mathematical/ aptitude and attainment for navigational understanding.

7. INTERESTS:

(a) Wide background interests — the possession of one particular hobby of a kind which can be taken up and left at short notice is an advantage. No particular hobby is preferable — merely any one which fits the conditions.

(b) Should like responsibility and prefer an extremely active mental life.

(c) Possibly travel — but not extreme or essential.

(d) Genuine interest in flying as a career.

8. PERSONALITY REQUIREMENTS:

(a) A person who is very stable emotionally is required. It is very important that a pilot should not be liable to crack under strains and stresses.

(b) Possessing the following "command" or "leadership" qualities which will equip him not only for success as a second pilot but later as a captain in command: dependability, initiative, keenness, ability to inspire confidence, calmness, self-discipline, good appearance, and bearing. Decisiveness, adaptability, co-operation, commands respect, sense of humour, breadth of outlook.

[These qualities are used as assessment variables for another part of the selection procedure. Without a full selection programme some might form part of the critical requirements of the interview. In this case we are assuming that, as in the real life situation upon which it is based, these leadership traits were assessed by group methods. See Shouksmith, 1958.]

9. SATISFACTIONS AND PROBLEMS. The job offers high salary and high status. There is the genuine satisfaction of flying. The pilot exercises control and responsibility to an

extensive degree. Offers little satisfaction to the person seeking stability above all. The pilot who is narrow in outlook — the "stick pusher" type — finds great difficulty in succeeding.

10. SOCIAL AND GENERAL:

(a) The successful pilot tends to be socially acceptable to his fellows and to the public and the Corporation executives alike. If he is married he must be prepared to be away from home for "night stops". His wife's views on the matter are found to be important since she must accept the lack of stability in her own life. For these reasons, too, the pilot should have a genuine interest in flying rather than regard it as a "glamour" job. The type who fall into the latter category tend to fail through an inability to adjust to the instability of the career.

(b) Although the pilot must be emotionally stable he must not be merely phlegmatic. Emotional stability is not sufficient in itself if the pilot is unable to make the correct decisions quickly.

From this analysis the critical requirements for the interview were isolated. The interview was restricted, as was the real life interview on which the case study was based, to a consideration of certain aspects only. Technical matters were dealt with separately and, as was mentioned in the analysis, the personality characteristics concerned with leadership were assessed through group interviews. Thus the critical requirements for the general assessment interview became:

(1) Emotional stability.

(2) Hobby or hobbies or outside interest of appropriate sort.

(3) Attitudes to job (attitude to taking responsibility and control).

(4) Interest in flying as a career (if married, wife's attitude to flying as a career is important).

(5) Acceptability on social and educational grounds.

Edward Saunders is one of the candidates who applies for the job. He appears to be satisfactory on the initial screening and is called in for interview. He has been asked previously to fill in an "interview questionnaire", which is shown in Table 4.1 (*overleaf*).

Mr. Elton, who interviews applicants on behalf of the Corporation, has perused this form and now proceeds to interview Mr. Saunders. The following is a transcript of the interview:

SECRETARY: "Come this way, Mr. Saunders, would you please — This is Mr. Elton."

MR. ELTON: "How do you do, Mr. Saunders. Do sit down, please. What I'd like you to do just now is to fill in some of the details for me about the things you put down on this form. You remember this?"

S. "Oh — yes."

E. "Good, well let's start right at the beginning with your schooling, shall we? This school, Bodlin, what sort of school was that?"

S. "Well, it was a private school really, rather a small one."

E. "A boarding school or a day school?"

S. "Both, though I was a day-boy — the school is just on the outskirts of Tordon, where my family lives."

E. "And how long were you at Bodlin school, Mr. Saunders?"

S. "I did all of my primary schooling there so I must have spent about six years there."

E. "Were you sorry to leave after all that time?"

S. "Not really — really quite glad I think."

E. "Why was that?"

S. "Oh, I suppose that as a day-boy in a school mainly consisting of boarders I felt a little out of it, and then day-boys tend to get picked upon."

E. "Was that the reason you then went to Tordon Grammar, rather than another private school?"

S. "I've never really thought — I suppose my parents knew I wasn't too happy at Bodlin and that might have had

TABLE 4.1. *Example interview questionnaire
for pilot selection case study*

NAME: Edward Saunders	AGE: 25 years

(1)   MAIN SCHOOL(S):   (1) Bodlin School;   (2) Tordon Grammer School.
      FAVOURITE AND BEST SUBJECTS: English and History, possibly French and
      languages.
      WORST AND DISLIKED SUBJECTS:
      EXAMINATIONS (Trade, G.C.E., etc.): G.C.E.O-Level, G.C.E. A-Level and
      County Major Bursary.

(2)   UNIVERSITY OR COLLEGE: University of Tordon
      COURSE TAKEN AND DETAILS: B.A. 2nd class honours in French with
      Subsidiary History and English.

(3)   SERVICE CAREER (GIVE DETAILS OF TYPE, e.g. NATIONAL SERVICE,
      SHORT SERVICE, ETC., FLYING EXPERIENCE AND DATES):
      (1) University Air Squadron 19   to 19   . Chipmunk jet trainers.
      (2) R.A.F. Short Service Commission 19   to present. Fighter Command, Mudley
      in Marsh — transferred Bomber Command, multi-engined planes at Adi-Alba,
      Middle East Command for 1 year. Back in England last 6 months.

(4)   JOBS (FULL OR PART-TIME, PRE- OR POST-SERVICE):

TITLE AND DUTIES	REASON FOR LEAVING

(5)   HOBBIES:

(6)   SPORTS: Golf.

(7)   INTERESTS: (UNDERLINE)

Reading	Dancing
History	Athletics
Science	Camping
Music	Mechanical
Painting	Voluntary service work

      OTHERS:

      DATE: . . . .   SIGNATURE: . . . .

something to do with it — but then Tordon was so near and such a good school so it may have been as simple as that."

E. "H-hm, Now, moving on a little, give me an outline would you of what you did in the G.C.E. exams; the subjects you took and how you did in them?"

S. "Well, let me see — at O-level I got credits in English, History, French and German and passes in Geography and Maths. I wasn't very fond of Maths, but at our school we had to do it whatever else we were doing."

E. "Do you think that's a good idea?"

S. "I didn't at the time, but now I find it very useful for my flying."

E. "And how about the A-level G.C.E.?"

S. "Oh, I advanced in English, History, and French — oh and I took an extra O-level subject in Spanish at the same time."

E. "It looks as though you were quite an expert at languages, Mr. Saunders — you didn't think of making a career in that line?"

S. "I suppose I did at one time — when I first went to Varsity I mean, though I don't think I was at all clear what I wanted to do just then."

E. "What reason had you for going on to Varsity then?"

S. "Oh — I suppose it was the done thing. My parents thought that whatever I did in life a university education would always be useful. Then most people I knew who had gone on to A-level in G.C.E. always went on to university — I suppose it would have been a bit of a waste of the sixth-form years if I hadn't."

E. "But at that time you had no specific career in mind — is that right?"

S. "Well I seem to remember I was vaguely thinking of teaching, or perhaps the Diplomatic Service if I got a good enough degree. But it was all very much in the air, and then I joined the University Air Squadron."

E. "And that changed everything?"

S. "It did rather — I caught the bug and then when it came round to my leaving Varsity I just applied for a short-service commission — flying was the only thing I wanted to do. In a way, I think flying accounts for my only getting a second — at least all my tutors said so."

E. "How did you come to join the University Air Squadron, Mr. Saunders?"

S. "It's quite funny really when I look back on it — I was just reading through the *Student Handbook* — the thing that tells you about all the various activities — and I'd been wondering what to do. You need some outside activities, and I wasn't all that keen on athletics or the social clubs for that matter. The Air Squadron seemed a good idea — you know the youngsters' idea on these things — zooming about the skies and all that. I thought it was very glamorous in those days too."

E. "You say you thought it was glamorous then?"

S. "Yes, well you know what youngsters are like about flying. It was very glamorous in the early days too — but a close friend of mine got killed, you see — it sort of changed things. Oh, it was his own fault, he'd been larking about just as we all did and something went wrong — that took the glamour away for me; I began to take flying much more seriously after that."

E. "But it didn't stop you going on flying?"

S. "No — I suppose flying sort of gets under your skin, it's a fascinating job. But the accident did make me think again; I began to realize that there's quite a lot of responsibility involved even in throwing a Tiger Moth about the skies — I suppose, too, that it was just about then I began to think of flying as something more than just a part-time game."

E. "Which year of your university training would this be?"

S. "The second."

E. "Tell me something now about your Air Force service, Mr. Saunders, would you please? Just give me an outline of where you went and what happened."

S. "Mm — first of all we did extended training — we didn't get much time on jets in the University Squadron. Then I was posted to Fighter Command, Mudley in Marsh. I was there for the rest of my first two years and then was posted out to Adi-Alba in the Middle East. Just about then I applied for a transfer to Transport Command."

E. "Why was that?"

S. "Well, whilst I was in Mudley I got married and then neither my wife nor I liked the move out to the Middle East; she managed to join me later, but it made us think. If I stayed in the Air Force and was posted around like that and we had any kids it would make home life rather difficult. So we began to think of alternatives. My wife wanted me to come out, but I wanted to stay flying. It must have been just about then I really began to think of civil aviation as a career. Then I thought I'd have a better chance of getting into an airline if I had experience, so I applied for a transfer to Transport Command. As it happens I didn't get it, but I did get put on to strategic bombers — multi-engined stuff, so I got my experience."

E. "You say that neither you nor your wife liked the idea of a lack of stability in your home life. How about civil aviation? We have night stops at various places, you know."

S. "To be quite honest, that's one reason why I chose this particular airline — it's all short-distance stuff, so one can't be away from home much longer than two or three nights at a time — besides, you've got to make some allowances to get what you want."

E. "Good, well let's move on — I see you put nothing down under hobbies — how do you fill your spare time?"

S. "Well, with flying and getting married, I don't seem to have had much really, but I think you could say that reading and music take the place of hobbies for me."

E. "Is that listening to music or performing it?"

S. "Both actually — I play the piano and then we go to concerts quite a lot."

E. "I see golf is your major sport, Mr. Saunders, did you start that at university or before?"

S. "Before, really, I used to play some at school."

E. "What else did you play at school, Mr. Saunders?"

S. "Oh, all the usual things, rugby and cricket. I wasn't very good at them though, I never made a school team or anything, though I did quite well at swimming."

E. "You were quite good at swimming, were you?"

S. "I got into the school team all right and won the local free-style championship, but I never went beyond that. That was one good thing about being out at Adi-Alba, though, we got some grand swimming. I must say that if I get this job I shall quite look forward to spending some time off on the Med. route so that I can get a swim in."

E. "Yes, perhaps there are compensations to these night stops. Well, Mr. Saunders, I think that's all I want to cover just now. Thank you very much for your co-operation. Perhaps if you would go back to the waiting room just now, then our secretary will call you for the next part of the procedure. Good morning."

Discussion

The interview is not perfect; it was not intended to be, but rather to mirror what happens in practice, which rarely if ever matches perfection. All case studies of this type should leave room for discussion and speculation and this one was designed with this in mind. When it has been used in a practical course on interviewing the general opinion has been that it is quite an effective interview. Course members have always felt, however, that there have been certain areas where the interviewer failed to cover the ground adequately. Some point to the information on marriage and argue that the interviewer failed to follow up sufficiently the question of Saunder's wife's attitude to flying as a career. This, they maintain, makes it impossible for them to rate adequately relevancy number 4. Others point to different areas which they feel should be more fully investigated, though most of those who have heard the interview in its taped form agree that it is *in general* effective. I would suggest that the reader makes his own assessment of the interview, perhaps producing his own list of faults or omissions and strong areas.

It may also be of interest to compare the assessments of the candidate made by a group of administrative and personnel officers with your own opinion. The method of assessment used was to rate the candidate in terms of each critical requirement on a five-point scale. The scale used was as follows and the ratings given appear in Table 4.2:

A. Strongly recommended for acceptance in terms of this requirement.
   Shows high possession of qualities concerned.
B. Recommend.
C. *Either* One cannot say on the evidence available;
   or In terms of this requirement, the candidate neither possesses it to a degree sufficient to recommend him, nor lacks it sufficiently to cause his rejection.
D. Not recommended.
E. As far as this requirement is concerned, the candidate's standing in it is at such a level as to suggest his definite rejection.

TABLE 4.2. *Ratings given to the candidate by eleven course members on the five critical requirements of the pilot selection case study*

Critical requirement	Rater no.										
	1	2	3	4	5	6	7	8	9	10	11
A	2	2	1	3	2	2	2	3	2	2	1
B	2	3	2	2	2	2	2	2	2	2	2
C	2	2	2	3	2	2	2	2	1	1	2
D	3	3	3	4	2	3	2	4	2	2	2
E	2	2	2	3	1	2	1	3	2	2	2

In general there was agreement about the candidate's standing on the various measures. On the second critical requirement there is 100% agreement, about 70% on number 4, and somewhat over 80% on all the others. It is quite possible that a general inflating of the results took place which in squashing all ratings at the top end of the scale made them appear to be in greater agreement than they were in fact. Over the years different courses have assessed the candidate in different ways. The overall impression gained, however, has usually been of an acceptable candidate who has some weak areas and about whom we just do now know enough to rate adequately on critical requirement number 4.

CHAPTER 5

"Odds" and "Ends" about Interviewing

So far I have attempted to provide a systematic action plan for improving interviewing. At this stage there still remains much to be said about various minor factors which affect the interview and about facets of interviewing which do not readily fall within the schematic plan of the first four chapters. I am, therefore, devoting this short section to a consideration of these various facets, all of which are, nevertheless, important to the topic under discussion.

Planning and Administering an Interview Programme

The first of the three factors which I mentioned in Chapter 3 as controlling the success of the interview concerned "the background initial work in organizing and planning the interview and the interview programme". Part of this is the isolation of critical requirements, but in addition such pedestrian steps as planning, timing, organizing, and administering the interview programme are also involved. There is no attempt being made in this book to provide an administrative text — knowing my own lack of efficiency in that direction I would not have the temerity to attempt it. The following few remarks, however, should, I feel, be made in order to remind people of these important and oft-forgot aspects of "good" interviewing.

Paper Work

The preparation and distribution of any necessary forms should obviously be completed before the day and time of the interview itself. Papers and forms including pre-interview questionnaires belonging to any particular candidate should be kept in that candidate's file. When the interviewer comes to make the actual interview he should have on his desk only one file — that of the candidate he is about to see. There is nothing more annoying both to candidate and interviewer than for the latter to have to search around under piles of papers in order to find the correct file. For the interviewer it is embarrassing too, which will naturally affect his performance.

Physical Setting

Quite frequently the interview is relegated to whatever room happens to be vacant at the moment, be this the Managing Director's office, complete with its full quota of paper and "untouchable" matter, or the cupboard under the stairs. Ideally a separate room should be set aside for interviewing, but where this is not possible the interviewer's own room should be specially cleaned for the occasion. It is a moot point whether, if the candidate is for a "works" job, he should be interviewed in the engineer's office next to the familiar noise of the "shop" or in some remote personnel office which, though calm and unflurried, lends a slightly artificial tone to the prospective employee's surroundings.

Wherever the room is, the layout of the furniture is probably more important. A desk and two chairs of approximate equality are required. If the candidate is perched on the edge of a hard-bottomed back-breaking upright seat while the interviewer reclines in padded luxury, the atmosphere is hardly conducive to obtaining that free style of interviewing advocated in Chapter 3. Although for some purposes, mainly clinical counselling, the reverse is advocated by some psychotherapists, my own preference is for a reasonably comfortable equality in chairs.

Furthermore, I feel that these chairs should not be placed on opposite sides of the desk or table so that candidate and interviewer, unless they wish to be grossly rude, are compelled to stare or glare at one another. If candidate and interviewer are opposed to one another physically, it so often seems to lead to an emotional or mental opposition which is detrimental to the success of the interview. Figure 5.1 shows my own preference, as it breaks down the formal setting to just the right degree. Interviewer and candidate can talk naturally to one another without any physical barrier and yet there is desk room for the interviewer to keep private any confidential papers or notes he wishes to take, and the setting allows a nervous candidate to let his gaze wander without seeming impolite.

Many prefer not to have a desk at all, feeling that this approach brings a welcome degree of informality to what can be a stressful situation. One must remember that the interviewer needs to be, and feel, relaxed, otherwise he will not be able to take an appropriately relaxed orientation to the interview. For this reason, the individual interviewer's own preferences should dictate the physical setting chosen providing this choice serves to break down the formal opposition of questioner and questioned.

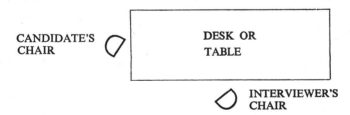

FIG. 5.1. Plan of suggested layout of furniture for interviewing.

Reception

I remember some years ago being in the position of candidate for a particular job. I arrived at the appropriate place at somewhere around the appropriate time and, looking back, rather self-importantly announced my name. The receptionist looked blank — she had never heard of me. A visit down the corridor, however, confirmed that my fears that I had arrived perhaps on the wrong day were unfounded. A candidate can easily be upset by such treatment, and perhaps an acceptable one may well decide, after such treatment, that he does not want this job after all. In present-day industry the employer must sell himself too.

The receptionist or secretary should be given a list of applicants who are to be seen on a given day with their times of arrival. The complete process which is assessment interviewing can then begin in the right way with the candidate having been received in a correct and proper fashion.

Waiting Facilities

The same firm whose reception methods I criticized had one other fault. There was no waiting room and I was left standing in the corridor gathering draughts and the curious stares of passers-by. Somewhere where candidates can await their interview in relative comfort is essential, even if attention to the next section reduces waiting to a minimum.

Timing

Leaving candidates to wait for any length of time is an offence. Frequently a candidate has to wait for many minutes or even an hour because the interviewer has got behind in his interviews. This usually happens because the interviewer tries to see too many candidates in one day or one morning. Probably he was a little late in starting so that he did not see the first candidate till 10 minutes after his due time. This delayed the second interview in consequence and then because the second candidate proved a difficult one to assess, it took the interviewer an extra 5 minutes to complete the write up properly. The third interview went on far too long, at least an extra 15 minutes, as some interviews just seem to do. The interviewer, himself, beginning already to feel a little jaded, felt he had to take 10 minutes off to snatch a cup of tea. Thus the fourth candidate, arriving on time, had to wait about 40 minutes before the interviewer was ready for him. Both interviewer and candidate being worried about this state of affairs, it is doubtful if further assessments made that day would retain their satisfactory nature.

The answer to this problem is simple and may be stated in terms of a number of steps:

Step 1. Never attempt to see more than about six to eight candidates in one day. It is doubtful if you can handle more without mental fatigue occurring, even if the timing allows them.

Step 2. Allow time for perusing each candidate's application and forms before seeing him and for completing any written assessment before seeing the next candidate. A 10-minute period between interview times should allow for both these.

Step 3. Place a tea break in the programme so that you are not forced to squeeze this in between interviews.

Usher

In many cases the interviewer has to bring his own candidates to the interview room. A secretary or receptionist who takes the candidate to the interviewer and who can introduce one to the other seems preferable. This is probably not a hard and fast rule, however, and there are some interviewers who prefer to go to the waiting room and collect the candidate. They then use the walk down the corridor to "break the ice", as it were. For my own part I feel that any value to be gained by this is lost in the necessary shuffling of chairs and manoeuvring involved in sitting down once the interview room is reached.

Duration

The question is often asked: How long should an interview last? The easy answer to this one is as long as you need to extract all the information you require. In practice this complete freedom from any worries about timing is impossible, and in many respects not desirable, since an overlong interaction will tend to loose direction. Different people will require various lengths of interview to bring them out and the status level of a particular job will dictate how much time and money an employer will put into the selection of an individual for that job. For these reasons, no hard and fast rules can be made as to the exact duration which any interview should take. As a guide to appropriate durations of interviews for various types and levels of jobs or positions, the following few examples might be of interest:

(1) In selecting women for training as skilled operatives in a tailoring factory, an interview of 20 minutes is used and appears to be successful.

(2) For the selection of cadets for the N.Z. Forest Service, some of whom will train as Rangers in the Forest Service's own training schools and some of whom will be given bursaries to attend university, an interview of 30 minutes has been chosen.

(3) For the selection of airline pilots a time-table which allowed for a maximum of 45 minutes for each interview was used.

In general, a good average figure for a single interview is round about 30 minutes. This allows sufficient time to get the candidate talking and to get him or her to provide the information you want about their attitudes, feelings, and behaviour habits. For senior positions the time given to any one candidate in any one interview may be extended, though it is doubtful if beyond about 50 minutes you are getting much additional information which could be useful. It would probably be better to give the candidate a second interview if you felt the need to go beyond this since both your own fatigue as interviewer and his as candidate would begin to affect the results. At the other end of the scale, even with the most junior, "low-status" positions within the organization, it is doubtful if an interview of less than 15 minutes would be of much use except to judge appearance and surface manner.

Processing Paper Work

Immediately following each assessment interview the interviewer should rate the candidate he has just seen on the critical requirements which form the specific assessment task. In addition it is a useful *aide-mémoire* to write a short pen-picture of the interviewee, highlighting any significant findings which emerged from the interview.

All paper work on a whole group of candidates should be processed on the same day that they are interviewed. If left till the following day other work piles up to confuse the picture and memory defects lead to forgetfulness of just what should go where and what was agreed to the previous day.

Board versus Individual Interviews

All that I have said so far has implied the use of one interviewer interviewing one candidate. I have not been concerned at all with Board interviewing and the omission has been deliberate. It is, in fact, my opinion that most of the evils of interviewing are to be found mainly in the Board interview. Board interviews seem to bring out the worst in every interviewer and many an interview has been used by a member of the Board merely to display his own knowledge or as a means of scoring off the candidate. This is, I realize, a criticism of particular Boards, but it is my experience that this so often happens that I feel a closer, critical look at Board interviewing is required.

In fact, on a number of grounds a good case *against* Board interviewing can be made out. Assessment in an interview is made through controlled interaction and to be successful the interaction must be adequately controlled. When a candidate first comes into the interview, he, just as much as the interviewer, is testing out the situation. During the first part of the interview both participants are concerned with exchanging attitudes and settling down. The candidate comes to the interview with his own attitudes and expectancies and he has to settle down before the interviewer can begin to assess him. The interviewer in his turn has to allay any fears the candidate might have and at the same time probe the candidate's behaviour to see how best to handle the conversation. During this settling down period, little useful information is acquired. With one interviewer it takes time for this settling down to occur for any initial anxieties to be allayed. If not one, but three, four, or five interviewers are involved, it is sometimes doubtful if the interview ever progresses beyond this initial stage to find out anything about the real person.

In the previous chapters I have stressed the need to control the interview in the correct manner to lead the conversation through to the conversation's purpose. This is difficult enough with only one interviewer and is much more so where a Board is involved. Here no one person controls the whole interaction; the control shifts as each Board member takes up the interviewing. Sometimes the control fails, the interview gets out of hand, and the purpose is lost. I remember one occasion where for about 5 or 10 minutes three of the Board members argued among themselves over some obscure point. The candidate was able to sit back and relax, very sensibly leaving it to them.

These views are not merely personal prejudice as I have some slight experimental evidence to show that Board interviews are inferior. In the field of engineering apprentice selection I compared the results of the selection of thirty boys as made by a three-man Board interview and by two individual interviewers. Follow-up of the selected boys' progress and reports made of the boys' ability, behaviour, and potential by their training supervisors, indicated that the individual interviews of about 30 minutes' duration each provided much wider and more valuable information about the candidates than did a three-man Board interview. The additional person in the Board interview and the capabilities of the various interviewers must be taken into account, but in general the results are in favour of individual interviews.

Theoretically, too, a reasonable argument may be made in favour of individual interviews. The outcome of an interview depends for its success on how the interviewer handles the twofold relationship between himself and the candidate. When that relationship is fourfold, or fivefold, as it would be in even a reasonably sized Board interview, it must become so much more difficult to handle it successfully.

There will always be those who prefer the Board interview; some may lack the courage of their own convictions and need the support of other Board members for any decision as to a candidate's worth; others may feel unable to hold a conversation with the candidate if on their own for more than, say, 5 minutes, and so prefer to share the load. Whatever the reason, Board interviews are still popular, although my own advice would be akin to that famous advice given to those about to be married – "Don't".

In fact there are many occasions when a Board interview, but not necessarily an assessment interview by a Board, is essential if not desirable. If a committee or council are responsible for a particular post, then the whole committee may need to see and approve a candidate. In a complex selection process where two or more assessors collect data from a variety of assessment tests and exercises, including one or more individual assessment interviews, a final Board interview by the panel of selectors may prove a useful summary tool. In these and other examples where Board interviews are used, the interview becomes part of the "decision-making" process rather than a separate assessment. At the end of a complex selection procedure the assessors may wish to refresh their memory of the candidate. A Board with the executive responsibility of making a selection decision may use an interview to see in the flesh the candidate recommended by their personnel consultant. In an interview the Board can compare earlier impressions or use the time as a final chance to allow the candidate to tell them about anything he thinks is important but which he has not as yet had a chance to tell anyone about. The Board can use the interview to dispel any false impressions either way. In all these "purposes" it is not so much assessment as clarification and integration of impressions which is occurring. And for this purpose the Board interview may effectively be used.

CHAPTER 6

Background and Development

Relatively new among selection techniques is that of group selection or group interviewing. This is not to be confused with Board interviewing where a number of interviewers assess one candidate at a time. Group interviewing refers to those situations where a number of candidates are assessed together whilst carrying out some task or discussion. This type of assessment situation has been referred to by names such as socio-drama, social interaction, group situation, or group task analysis, all of which have in common the fact that they are concerned with assessing individuals as "going wholes". In referring to these situations as group interviews, I am emphasizing the similarity with the more common interview, the "conversation" aspect. In industrial group selections, the basis of this technique is normally a group discussion of some kind and this forms the conversation upon which assessment is based. The two techniques are not identical since in the individual interview the interviewer takes a very strong role in the conversation whereas in the group "interview" he is outside, as it were, observing and listening to the candidates' discussion.

In recent years, applied social science's greatest impact on society has undoubtedly been in the human relations training and T-group movements, which aim at fostering planned change through the use of groups (e.g. Bion, 1948; Bennis *et al.,* 1961).

The basic tool used in these change programmes is the same as that used in group selection programmes, that is a group of individuals engaged in free multi-way interaction, usually directed towards some task. Such a group forms a dynamic entity in which each individual strives to express his own personality and in which the interacting forces of the group itself, produced by the need to direct efforts towards a common task, combine together to create what Lewin (1947) has referred to as a system in tension. This tension can be used to produce change in individual and social behaviour, or it can be used by the assessor to allow him to see through the façade of each job applicant to the real personality underneath. In the selection-assessment group each group member is trying to impress his personality on the group and to gain acceptance by the group of his points of view. The group interview, therefore, emphasizes the assessment of leadership qualities of the individual, the persuasive, directive ability of the candidate in competitive group situations.

This was the "purpose" of the first group selection techniques used in the English-speaking world, developed by the British Army in the early days of World War II. These first group selection techniques formed part of the War Office Selection Boards, or W.O.S.B's as they soon came to be known. At the beginning of World War II the Army selected its officers by the traditional methods of a Board interview for men who possessed a School Certificate and who had been members of an O.T.C. The vast and inconceivable demand for junior officers which the war produced, the losses through failures at O.C.T.U. and more seriously on the fields of battle, and the effects on morale of the use of these traditional methods, all combined to make it imperative that a new approach to the selection of officers be made. Since the actual role of a junior officer was to lead a group of men, the rather novel approach to selection was made of taking candidates in groups and observing how they coped as members of the group — whether they appeared as leaders or followers. Thus was born the War Office Selection Board where candidates lived together, performed tasks together, solved problems, and discussed topics together over a period of time. The whole assessment procedure, which included tests and individual interviews, had an overall aim which was stated by Morris (1949) to be an attempt to obtain a fairly comprehensive acquaintance with the candidate both as an individual and as a member of a group. During the selection programme the candidates were asked to perform certain practical tasks, to plan certain projects, to perform in team judgement exercises, and carry out group discussions on various topics. These were the group aspects of the whole selection programme and, together with the rest, they produced assessments which proved to be more satisfactory than older techniques when judged against failure rates at O.C.T.U. or the opinion of commanding officers assessing successful candidates' later service records.

Although practical tasks which involved such activities as getting a mock gun carriage over a ditch without letting it, or any human member of the team for that matter, fall in, might be suitable for the selection of military leaders; it could hardly be regarded as a necessary skill for industrial managers or office executives. The mind boggles at the thought of some grey-suited young executive, in matching shirt and socks, with contrasting tie, arriving as candidate for a managerial position in some large company and leaving in horror on being led to an adjacent and muddy field and being presented with some rather grubby practical task. But the W.O.S.B. scheme, in its group discussions and verbal projects, did provide excellent material for use with civilian populations. This was shown when certain group interviews were included with more formal and traditional paper-and-pencil examinations and tests in the new Civil Service Selection Boards (Wilson, 1948). A committee of three consisting of the chairman of the Selection Board and an observer, both of whom were full-time civil servants of a senior grade, and a psychologist, was formed to assess the group periods and to rate the candidates on them. The candidates were asked to take part in a group discussion, to sit on a committee, and to handle and expound on certain problems in committee. These exercises were designed to resemble the sort of work which a higher civil servant might be called upon to do.

In Britain such techniques were applied to industrial use in areas as wide apart as, on the one hand, a coal distribution organization (Fraser, 1950) and, on the other, pilot selection (Shouksmith, 1960b). In South Africa, Arbous (1953) developed a comprehensive programme for the selection of administrative trainees in a large industrial corporation, the basis of which was a battery of group interviews or tasks. Apart from reported studies, a whole host of "house parties", "group selections", "conference assessments", etc., were and are being used throughout the commercial world for the selection of managerial and supervisory staff. As with many individual interviews, so many of these tend to be unsystematic, biased in their assessments, and generally unreliable and invalid. In some, the observers are impressed by the verbal types who have what in slang terms is described as "the gift of the gab". In others, the assessors appear unaware of exactly what qualities they require in applicants or of exactly what is entailed in the job.

It is hardly surprising, therefore, that the same criticisms which arose with some individual interviews were levelled at group selections. And yet the system can provide information about a candidate's potential performance as a member of a group which it is virtually impossible to obtain by other techniques. Hence what is required is a system such as the one we applied to the individual interview which will control its reliability and validity and restrict its bias.

To achieve adequate results in the individual interview, I suggested in Chapter 3 that there were certain basic areas which must be attended to. These were summarized as:

(1) The background, initial work in organizing and planning the interview, and the interview programme.

(2) The orientation and attitude of mind which the interviewer has both to the interview and to the candidate who has to be assessed.

(3) The method of conducting the interview which the

interviewer has, his manner with the candidate, and his ways of obtaining information.

The first of these requirements refers to the organization and planning of the interview programme as covered in Chapter 5 and, more importantly, to the establishment of critical requirements forming the "special purpose" of the interview. For group interviews a method of assessing the interaction which takes place in the group must be arranged. The assessments should be in a form which can be related to critical requirements emerging from the job analysis and of factors which can be identified through group interaction (e.g. leadership attributes).

The second factor, the orientation of the interviewer, virtually remains the same whether the interview in question is individual or group. The assessor in group interviews should follow the "rules of orientation" in the same way that the individual interviewer does. These define for the assessor a way of approaching his assessment task and the attitudes he should take to interactions he observes in the group. To summarize again, the important rules of orientation and to isolate those particularly relevant to assessors of group interviews, these are:

(1) Above all else, to listen, but to listen intelligently and critically.

(2) To interpret what is said as throwing light on each group member's skills, nature, or personality. The aspects of the individual which will be most readily revealed will usually be command or leadership qualities.

The final requirement draws attention to the need for the interviewer to control the interview, directing it towards throwing light on the specific purpose of the interview. In group selection techniques the assessor is a non-participant observer and so cannot directly influence the interaction once it is in progress. Control can only be exercised by setting specific tasks for the group to perform or guidelines within which the interactions must take place. The tasks and guidelines are derived from the "special purpose" isolated for the group interview, and provide the control which is required over the course of the interaction process. In practice, this control is achieved by the form of briefing given to the discussion participants and by the questions which are raised for discussion, the nature of the exercises, and projects set as the group tasks. In this way the conversations and interactions of the group are directed into appropriate channels.

CHAPTER 7

Organizing and Operating a Group Interview Programme

The newcomer to group investigation is often surprised at the extent to which group participants under observation reveal themselves. They are not always on guard, and through their interactions with their fellows, participants show themselves in their many guises as, often unpredictable, warm or cold, rational or irrational, but always interesting, human beings. The raw material for his observations, particularly in leaderless groups, will undoubtedly be, as Mills (1964) points out: "disorderly and often incoherent . . . confused by lack of order and pattern." The observer quickly develops a feel for the group, but, as with the individual interview, if bias and prejudice are to be kept in check, his assessments need to be systematized. At least two approaches may be identified for the systematic assessment of individual behaviour in groups. One is based directly on the overt behaviour of the participants, what is said and done in the group and can be directly observed. The second approach focuses on the covert feelings or unexpressed thoughts which lie behind the expressed statements; this approach makes a direct assessment of the personality of the individual as it is revealed through interaction in the group. Both methods have their advantages and disadvantages. The first, focusing on overt, observed verbal actions of each participant, gives a first-stage categorization of behaviour which is at least arguably objective. To get from the semi-objective first analysis to an assessment of individuals in terms of selection criteria, however, requires a second interpretational phase which is either subjective or statistically complex *and* limited to a small set of personal characteristics. The second method suffers from being largely impressionistic and subjective. It has the advantage, however, of providing one-stage immediate assessments of personal characteristics. If these characteristics are carefully predefined and the assessor follows the "rules" for group interviewing, then these semi-subjective assessments of group participants can, like their counterparts in individual interviewing, be both reliable and valid.

Let us look at each of these approaches in turn.

Interaction classification assessment

The group discussion can be regarded as being formed from a series of individual contributions. Each of these will be determined in part by the fact that the member making that contribution *is* a member of the group. Group members will try to make their own positions known, try to impress their own attitudes on the group, or respond to contributions from others. Thus the discussion is a complex series of interactions which can be analysed in terms of individual single "behaviours". In group interviews the behaviours in question will be verbal in nature, taking the form of sentences, words, grunts, or groans. Most interaction analyses ignore non-verbal communications in the form of nods, winks, frowns, and so on, because of the high degree of inference or interpretation as to what they are, which they require of the observer. Assessments made of group participation based on interaction classification, therefore, focus on the individual verbal comments or contributions of each participant. A comment is usually recorded only if it expresses at least one complete thought. This limitation helps in deciding whether non-sentence length comments should be recorded. For example, the comment "Yes" would be recorded and classified, but the comment: "Well, ah . . ." would not.

The aim of classifying the participants' contributions is to determine what precisely is going on in the group. In doing this we can, as Schein (1969) has pointed out, concentrate on the content of the interactions as they relate to the group task, or we can focus on the interaction process itself, in terms of the style of the communications observed, who speaks to whom, etc. In practical or assessment terms this distinction is similar to Benne and Sheats' (1948) suggestion that behaviour in the group can be viewed in terms of what its purpose or function is. Some of the comments or contributions will have a task function, and others a group maintenance function, since if it is to achieve its goal the group has to be maintained as an interacting entity. Amongst the participants making positive contributions to the interaction, one can isolate two kinds of leaders, as Bales (1950) has pointed out. These are the task leaders who try to steer the group towards successful completion of its task and socio-leaders who attempt to create and maintain harmony in the group. Bales arrived at these conclusions from data derived from a series of group discussions and exercises, the interaction processes in which were classified in terms of a twelve-category scheme which he devised. Bales' findings illustrate a simple practical possibility for assessment of participants in group interviews. By setting the group an appropriate task, one, for example, which is related to or simulates performance on the job for which candidates are being assessed, the observer can, from the tally of each participant's interactions, judge his relative performance as a task and/or socio-leader in a relevant situation. The simpler the categorization scheme the more reliable classifications of interactions are likely to be. If one selects an appropriate and relevant group task, a scheme which provides a direct score in the major leadership cagegories is all that is required. By combining Bales' scheme with the functional role categorization made by Benne and Sheats, one can derive the following simple direct observation categorization scheme (Table 7.1).

During the group interview, the observers simply categorize each comment or contribution as one of the four major categories listed. A tally is kept of each participant's contributions to the interaction process, using a tally sheet like that shown in Table 7.2.

TABLE 7.1. *Four-category assessment scheme*

Category	Identifying behaviour
A. Task behaviour — Directive (directing or task-oriented group-directing behaviour)	1. Initiates new line of discussion 2. Gives information or opinion 3. Clarifies, elaborates, or summarizes
B. Task behaviour — Searching (task-oriented interactions attempting to establish status of group goal-oriented activity)	1. Seeks information or opinions 2. Consensus testing 3. Asks for direction or for further interaction
C. Social group behaviour — positive (behaviour which is group-supportive and enhances group cohesion)	1. Encourages, rewards and gives help to others 2. Harmonizing — brings members together — jokes, laughs 3. Compromising, lessens differences, shows understanding
D. Social group behaviour — negative (activities which are non-supporting of the group or even disruptive)	1. Shows rigid, non-participative behaviour; won't interact 2. Shows an antagonism, asserts self, deflates others 3. Takes independent line, disagrees, will not help others

From the example work sheet shown in Table 7.2 one can see that the strongest participant was No. 3, with Nos. 6, 1 and 2 also being strong group members. No. 3 showed more directive task behaviour than the others, but also contributed a fair number of disruptive comments. The suggestion is that he is strongly directive and task-oriented, but may at times put self above the group. No. 6, on the other hand, as well as being task-directive is also highly group-supportive. He shows, therefore, a well-balanced task and maintenance approach to the group. At the other end of the scale No. 4 is seen as a neutral, grey person, whilst No. 5, although more participative, is predominantly disruptive. It is interesting to note that the method also distinguishes different approaches to task leadership. No. 2, for

TABLE 7.2 *Example work sheet for observation analysis*

COMMENT CATEGORY	Participant					
	1	2	3	4	5	6
A	1111 1111 1111 (14)	1111 11 (7)	1111 1111 1111 1111 (24)	1111 (4)	1111 11 (7)	1111 1111 111 (18)
B	1111 1111 11 (12)	1111 1111 1111 (19)	1111 1111 (10)	1111 1 (6)	1111 1111 (9)	1111 1111 (10)
C	1111 1111 1111 1 (16)	1111 1111 1111 (15)	1111 1111 (9)	1111 111 (8)	11 (2)	1111 1111 11 (17)
D	1 (1)	11 (2)	1111 1 (6)	11 (2)	1111 1111 111 (13)	1 (1)
TOTAL PARTICIPATION	43	43	49	20	31	46

example, seems to favour the "Socratic" method, directing the group through searching behaviour. No. 1's spread of scores also seems to illustrate that "leadership" is not confined to one person in the group and is, indeed, a relative phenomenon. Experienced observers may wish to develop a more sophisticated categorization system which can readily be produced by using the "identifying behaviours" listed in Table 7.1, which are derived from Bales' original twelve, as subdivisions of the four major categories.

Direct Assessments of Individual Characteristics

Interaction process assessments provide direct content analyses of contributions to the group discussion. To give meaning to the category tallies for each participant as indicators of his personal qualities still requires interpretation from the assessor. For this reason, observer—assessors of group interviews may well prefer to make direct assessments of the individual participants in terms of what their contributions reveal of the participant's own individual characteristics and skills. Evidence suggests that if the observer—assessor clearly understands the nature of the characteristics he is rating and their behavioural concomitants, assessments of this kind can be useful and reliable. In theoretical studies, for example, Schein (1969) has shown that individuals display characteristic styles of participation, which for them both reduce tension and express their motivation and emotional needs. Schein isolates three "pure types" of group participant – the "tough battler", the "friendly helper", and the "logical thinker". Schein shows how these participative styles can be related to the kind of group in which the participant prefers to work, the constructs he uses in evaluating other people's behaviour, and his preferred method of influencing others. This analysis seems most helpful in analysing groups which are attitude change, action, or general personal development groups. For the selection group a similar direct attribute rating method, but one related to the critical requirements of the selection task, seems more generally appropriate.

The Trait-Rating Method

The basis of the trait-rating method is to have a number of competent judges choose the qualities required for leadership in the particular situation under study. Each candidate is then rated for his performance in the group interviews on each of these qualities or traits. The overall judgement in terms of these traits is then taken as the rating of leadership potential for that candidate in that particular situation. How the list is produced may well vary from situation to situation, although the first stage in its production will be identical with that used in the case of individual interviews.

A general job analysis is made and if this indicates that supervisory, executive, managerial, or other leadership requirements exist, then the use of group techniques may be advocated and a trait list be prepared. One of the best ways of doing this in practice is to use a group interview or discussion for the purpose. If a group of people who are familiar with the job in question are brought together, they can, through discussion, arrive at a list of the traits needed. The best way of approaching the task is for the group discussing the requirements to talk about particular instances of good and bad leadership. At this stage, even if the discussion degenerates into a number of vague reminiscences of the variety " . . . I remember old so-and-so when he was in this job. He used to . . .", then it is not a bad thing at all. This not only helps to clear people's minds, but may have the further advantage of suggesting particular areas of importance for leaders in this job.

After the general discussion they can then, in a second session, say, work through the trait list given in Chapter 2, considering the various traits to see whether or not they are necessary requisites for leaders in that particular job. If there is a good majority of agreement, then the trait can be included in the list of critical ones.

Sometimes this procedure produces a list of mammoth proportions far too large to be used effectively by any assessor. In these cases a further refining of the list must be made. This can be achieved in a number of ways, just two of which are suggested below.

(1) A second small group of experts can re-assess the full list as produced from the earlier discussions and retain for the final list only those traits which are deemed essential by all the group.

(2) If a large number of people are available, all of whom have had experience of or are well acquainted with the job under discussion, then the original list may be given to this group in questionnaire form and they can be asked to rank or rate the traits in order of importance. The final list consists of those traits which by consensus of opinion are judged important. The size of this final list can, of course, be limited to any size you wish, simply by taking only a certain number of traits, working downwards from the top rating or top ranking.

In most cases the original analysis will be sufficient. The group can in fact be asked to limit its original list to a certain size — probably about ten or a dozen which seems to be an appropriate size list — to attain adequate coverage without overloading the observers. To simplify the task in a different way the second reduced list (should it prove necessary) may be produced by one person only — the personnel or administrative officer concerned.

Sometimes the whole process may, through force of circumstances, be placed in the hands of one man — the executive or administrator who is in charge of the selection. In these cases he would be wise to ensure the adequacy of his final list by consulting as many people as possible about the nature of the job concerned and its human requirements.

What has now been produced is a list of personality traits or characteristics to be looked for in the applicants, a list which is something akin to the critical requirements of the individual interview. The group interview assessor is now armed with a list of traits which are the traits required of leaders in the job for which they are assessing. As the group interviews progress they can then, on a basis of each candidate's performance in the group, rate him or her for the possession of the necessary traits to the given degree. This limited set of traits or characteristics serves to direct the observer's judgement, restricting his assessments so that personal prejudice and bias are kept to a minimum.

Various Types of Group Interview

Although I have been referring in general terms to *the* "group interview", this term — as for *the* individual interview — is probably a misnomer. Not only the tasks set the participants, but the ground rules under which interaction takes place, may be varied, so forming a variety of types of group interviews.

The Basic Group Interview – A Group Discussion

Since the more active, or empirical, group task is normally ruled out as far as applying group techniques to selection programmes in the commercial world, the group discussion becomes the basic method. In its simplest form it consists of a number of candidates sitting down together and as a group discussing some question or questions. These questions or discussion topics can be specific, technical, or general, and can be supplied by the assessor or the groups themselves. The group are assembled in a room which should be large and airy and decorated pleasantly. Various methods of seating the candidates may be used, all based on the "open square". The more common methods can be seen in Fig. 7.1. As you can see, the seating in Fig. 7.1 is in each case arranged for six candidates. This is neither an accident nor a coincidental arrangement dependent on the drawing space available. The best group size emerges as six; this being a size which is large enough to permit and encourage different viewpoints to be held, which encourages an effective discussion, and yet is not too large so that individual members of the group become lost. Furthermore, the optimum number I have given is based on empirical findings rather than an armchair analysis. Bernard Bass, who has carried out a great deal of admirable work on small groups, devoted one paper to the consideration of this specific point of optimum group size (Bass and Norton, 1951). This paper reported an experiment where the results obtained for leadership ratings in groups of various sizes were compared. The findings showed that the best-sized group, in terms of reliability of ratings achieved, was one of six members.

Normally two observers watch, listen, and assess the group interview. They are best referred to as observers since; except to give directions and instructions, they take no part in the discussion. Once the candidates are seated, the observer who is directing the group interview may begin briefing the candidates. His task at this stage is, first, to put the candidates at ease and then to give them directions as to how to proceed. He should make it clear that they are expected to discuss the topics among themselves and not address remarks to one or other of the observers. A good way to begin the discussion is to let the candidates themselves find a first topic. This enables the observers to see whose ideas are accepted at the outset — although one must be wary of judging everything on this first stage. As in the individual interview this is merely a warming-up stage and the discussions which occur later in the session may well be very different. If the candidates are instructed to find their own topic at the outset they should also be warned that at a later stage they will be given particular topics to discuss. The observer will usually interrupt the discussion by rapping on the table, so candidates should be warned that when they hear this they should for the moment stop talking and listen. Usually the discussion is best changed when it is still at its height, although a useful additional technique consists of allowing the odd discussion to come to a halt. It is then rather interesting to see which, if any, of the candidates are capable of getting the

(a) *Around a Table*

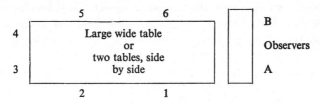

Chairs for candidates should have the spaces
between them all approximately equal.

(b) *Open Circle*

Candidates in open circle:

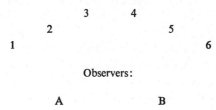

Observers:

A   B

Some people regard this method as having the
advantage of being slightly less formal.
Observers can use a "millboard" or have small
individual tables in front of them.

FIG. 7.1. Common methods of arranging candidates
for a group discussion.

discussion going again. This is only effective if tried occasionally, however, and changing the topic during an on-going discussion is normally recommended.

What topics are given for discussion will vary from situation to situation. During the ordinary group discussion, however, it is not normal to use many technical subjects, this session rather being used to assess general attitudes of the participants to political, social, and other everyday issues, light-hearted, and serious. The list given in the next chapter would probably do as a basic list for most situations to which specific job-related topics could be added, appropriate to the particular assessment task.

The Group Project

The second major technique which can be recommended for general use is the group project. This, like virtually all other group interviews, is merely a derivative of the group discussion. In the project, instead of a number of short questions of general interest being presented to the group, they are given an integrated problem or case study to discuss. For a varying period of, say, half an hour to an hour, the group concerns itself with hammering out the pros and cons of this complex problem. The project can be used to produce evidence on two major points. Firstly, a candidate's ability to appreciate the many aspects of a complex problem and to present and hold an integrated solution in discussion, can be compared with his prowess in general discussion. Secondly, the project can be used to assess the candidate's attitudes to, knowledge of, and ability to deal with specific and perhaps technical aspects of the job in question.

Projects can be of two kinds. They may be short in length, presenting a simple problem and giving few details for consideration. This type of project can be fitted into a half-hour session and allows candidates to display their knowledge and develop their own ideas. In contrast to this, the second type of project can be described as an integrated case study. This latter type is longer in length and usually requires a longer time for adequate use. As opposed to the first type, the case study project requires candidates to integrate facts as presented and to argue a case from the details given. Both types of projects naturally vary from situation to situation so that any example given here can only be used to illustrate the method in a general way.

Example: Short Project

The short project presented here is taken from a selection programme intended for use in the selection of an apprentice supervisor.

PROJECT

"A large engineering company are discussing the setting up of an apprentice training scheme. The Company consists of a main branch with one small subsidiary company in another centre. The main branch has two separate factories on different sites in the same town. As yet there is no Company training school.

"The aim of the apprentice training scheme may be stated as:

'To provide adequate training during the apprenticeship in order that the young man can obtain a job as a qualified craftsman or technician with the Company, or with another company should he wish to do so.'

"You are asked to discuss how such an apprentice scheme might operate. Pay particular attention to the content and form of training which you feel should be given and to how the scheme should be administered."

Example: Case study Project

This example is taken from a selection programme for a personnel officer. The particular field or personnel work in which this officer was to work would involve industrial relations, wages, etc. Hence the project was devised around these points.

CASE STUDY

"Twelve members of the staff were temporarily posted at the height of the holiday season to a base which was located at a seaside resort. All these staff were in receipt of the correct temporary posting allowances, which they had *elected* to receive for the duration of their posting and yet, on return, they all submitted 'hardship' claims on the basis that the allowances had been inadequate.

"The Facts
"(1)   When staff are temporarily posted, they can receive either the laid down temporary posting allowance or, if they think these will be insufficient, the firm will undertake to pay actual cost of approved accommodation in the area (including board and lodging costs).

"(2)   Investigation subsequently revealed that these staff had taken their wives and families with them and rented furnished bungalows and that accommodation was in any case very difficult to find and very expensive.

"(3)   Staff are not expected to take wives and families with them on temporary postings and no provision is made for this in the regulations.

"(4)   These staff all *elected* to receive temporary posting allowances.

"(5)   These temporary posting allowances are intended to cover board and lodgings at the temporary base.

"(6)   These postings ranged from three to five months' duration. When a posting is likely to exceed two months, the regulations state that the allowances to be paid should be assessed in advance. (These may well be in excess of what is normally paid.) This was not done on this occasion.

"(7)   Staff were informed before posting that assistance could be given in recommending addresses of suitable accommodation. This included a reference to bungalows in case staff decided to take wives. No liability was admitted or implied *re* subsistence for wives.

"(8)   The average temporary posting allowance paid was £9.50 ($18.00) per week. In view of the fact that it was during the height of the holiday season, the average cost of digs was between £10.0 ($18.00) and £20.0 ($36.00). The average cost of renting a bungalow was £13.50 ($25.00) to £27.50 ($50.00) per week.

"(9) Some of the items claimed for were as follows:

(a) Wages of domestic cleaner to look after the permanent home in the absence of the wife who had accompanied the staff member on temporary posting.

(b) Wages of a gardener to maintain the garden at the permanent home.

(c) Cost of sending dog to kennels, occasioned by the absence of the complete family.

(d) Compensation for higher cost of living in seaside resort.

(e) Taxi and bus fares incurred by family at temporary base.

(f) Cost of crockery and cutlery not provided with furnished accommodation.

(g) Extra cost of renting a bungalow.

(h) Cost of meals.

(i) Cost of delivery of fresh water to bungalow.

(j) Etc.

"(10) Staff are considered to be aware of the regulations governing temporary postings, which are published on staff notice boards and can be seen at any time by request.

"The Problem

"As a Committee you have been asked to discuss these various claims and say what action you would take. At the end of an hour you will be required to reach a decision and report your findings."

Although it has nothing to do with their inclusion in the project, readers will probably be interested to note that all the complaints and claims listed were taken from actual examples.

It is largely in the project that the directing of the candidates takes place, the direction which is for group interviews the counterpart of the control requirement which I noted for individual interviews.

Other Variations

In addition to varieties of the leaderless discussion, it is possible to run sessions where each candidate in turn takes the role of leader. Stress exercises where individuals or groups are placed under pressure to participate in a certain way or make rapid decisions which later they have to justify to the group, have all been tried at one time or another. All of these are derivatives from the two main procedures and are only of minor value. As with the individual interview, it seems that most value can be gained by a straightforward technique which encourages free interaction in a relatively stress-free and empathetic climate.

Note Taking

If you are not using a direct interaction classification, it is worth while making notes on the performance of the candidates during each exercise. Your final assessment can then be based on these notes as well as your general impressions. There are some users of group techniques who prefer not to make notes during the course of the interviews, saying that this will affect the outcome. It seems to me that since the observer is not part of the group and is seated separately from the group, what he does, providing he does it unobtrusively, should not affect the adequacy of the discussion. If you leave the full write-up of the discussion to the end, there is the further danger that your memory will play tricks with you and that your assessments will be based not so much on what actually happened as on what you remember, perhaps falsely, to have happened. Notes taken during the course of a discussion provide you, moreover, with further most useful material. If you make notes on the significant contributions, the behaviour patterns, the way of behaving of the various group members, you are then in a position at the end of the procedure not only to make ratings of traits, for example, but also to present useful pen-pictures of each candidate, summing up how they behaved in these group situations.

CHAPTER 8

A Practical Example of Group Selection

In the previous two chapters I have tried to indicate how group interviewing developed and to discuss its application to assessment work. One thing should be clear, and that is that group interviewing should not be used in isolation. Group methods have their chief use in the assessment of the personality aspects of leadership potential. To make clear how they are in fact utilized, I present in this chapter a complete account of a selection procedure for airline pilots, a major part in which is taken by group techniques. This will have the twofold purpose of showing how the methods described in the previous chapter operate in practice and also how they fit in with other assessments.

The Selection Task

In the summer of 1955 the national airline for which I was working at the time was faced with a great expansion of air travel and a consequent expansion of its own activities. Among the problems which this raised was the need to recruit and train a large number of pilots during the coming winter. Prior to this date few pilots had been recruited since the immediate post-war years when new recruits came from the ranks of ex-R.A.F. pilots, all of whom had considerable experience and whose capabilities could well be judged from their detailed log books. Hence these earlier recruits had been selected on the basis of a single 30-minute Board interview given by the Flight Managers. Even amongst these experienced men, however, a survey taken of the Flight Managers' views and of their actual performance suggested that this method of selection was not entirely satisfactory. In a report made at the time by myself and a senior member of the staff (Johnson and Shouksmith, 1956), it was concluded that "this method of selection did not in some cases assess properly (1) Command Potential, (2) Intellectual Capabilities, (3) Personal Qualities". The recruits anticipated in the new selection intake would all be young men without war-time experience, with a minimum of training, and mostly without a Commercial Pilot's Licence. It was, therefore, decided to review the existing system and it was deemed essential to introduce a comprehensive and thorough selection procedure for the new candidates.

The first step made was to review existing pilot selection systems currently in use by the major European airlines The R.A.F.'s procedures were also closely studied and, indeed, were of particular interest since they included group exercises based on W.O.S.B. procedures and it already seemed likely that these would be most useful in covering the assessment aspects concerned with what the Flight Managers called "Command Potential".

The next step consisted of holding a series of conferences with the Flight Managers of the Corporation. These themselves were interesting examples of the small group discussion but in this case used not for assessment but to "solve problems". From these conferences three salient factors emerged which were later to form the basis for the selection procedure. Firstly, given that a man knew how to fly, what was important on the technical side for success as an airline pilot was a sound technical-cum-engineering understanding. This was not so much knowledge as comprehension of technical matters, so that the pilot could, on the one hand, understand the technical aspects of how a modern complex airliner functioned and, on the other, could readily assimilate new data and techniques. Secondly, the personal qualities which were referred to by Flight Managers as being an essential possession of the successful airline Captain emerged as a sound and emotionally stable personality. An airline pilot is not called upon to be a daredevil wizard as many fictional and not a few factual pilots are. Rather his role is to be calm and unflurried, unemotional under difficulties, well adjusted to his role in life — in fact to be a perfectly normal and extremely stable chap. Thirdly, the conferences raised as a major issue the question of "Command Potential". Under the normal agreement with the Pilots' Association, promotion to captain was made on a basis of seniority. Thus, provided he maintained the requisite technical standards, each one of the junior pilots whom we were to select would one day hold a command position in the airline. With aircraft getting progressively larger, faster, and mote complex, the role of a captain in such craft would assume greater and greater importance, so that any selections we made would need to have a firm eye on leadership in the future.

The Selection Programme

In the early stages of the selection one or two different techniques were included in the programme only to be discarded once the results began to come through. The approach to intellectual assessment through paper-and-pencil aptitude and attainment tests, for example, was soon discarded since these tests were found not to discriminate at this level. Eventually, however, the programme settled down to a two-day procedure which is outlined in Table 8.1. The parts of this programme which are of particular interest to us here are the Group Discussion on the afternoon of day 1, and the Group Project, Chairmanship, or Command Exercises and Individual Situation Exercises which took place on the morning of day 2. Four separate assessments were made, two of which were on the results of the group interviews, the other two being by myself on the biographical interview and by a Flight Manager on the

TABLE 8.1. *Programme for two-day pilot selection procedure*

Day 1
  (1) *Assemble.* The Administrative Officer outlines the procedure and completes any administrative details necessary.

  (2) *Interview.* First interview with psychologist member of Board. Second interview with Flight Manager.
    (Lunch usually occurs during period 2.)

  (3) *Group discussion.*
  (4) (*Written project.* Omitted from later Boards.)

Day 2
  (1) *Group projects.* One or two of these.
  (2) *Chairmanship or command exercises.*
  (3) *Individual situation exercises.*
    (Lunch.)
  (4) *Final Selection Board.*

---

basis of a second interview which had a slightly more technical bias. This same Flight Manager, who undertook a course of training in assessment, also made one of the two ratings produced from the group sessions. Each of these four assessments were made on a five-point scale, A to E. These gradings were put in the form of concrete recommendations rather than semi-abstract terms. Thus A indicated that the candidate was strongly recommended, B that he was recommended, C a possible borderline, D not recommended, and E that he was definitely not recommended. In view of what I have said earlier about Board interviews it might be as well for me to say exactly what was expected of the Final Selection Board on this occasion. This Final Selection Board consisted of the General Flight Manager as chairman, the two assessors who had run the whole procedure, one other Flight Manager or Senior Captain, and a non-flying management member. In the case of clear-cut decisions, where the candidate's ratings were all Bs or As, or conversely were all Ds or Es, the F.S.B. merely confirmed the opinion of the assessors and accepted or rejected the candidate.

In these, the majority of cases, the F.S.B. acted as a ratifying Board, and in the legal sense, since its chairman was the General Flight Manager, acted as the body responsible for employing a given pilot. Where a mixture of ratings was obtained by a candidate or where all the ratings given were Cs, the F.S.B. had the additional task of weighing all the evidence as presented in the pen-pictures of any written reports on the candidate before producing a decision. The following quotation from the "Notes for Guidance" which were issued to Board members will, I think, make this position clear:

> " . . . it will be seen that the final Board interview is viewed not so much as an assessment interview but as a period when, using the assessments already made, the Board can make a final choice as to whether the candidate will be accepted or rejected. It is suggested that members of the Board ask questions of the candidates only on specific points which they feel are not clear and in cases where they feel there is some doubt in the previous assessments. . . ."

The Group Assessments

Those parts of the whole programme which are of interest to us here are the various group interviews or exercises. In order to make clear exactly how such exercises are used in practice, I have given a brief outline of each one below.

Group Discussion

Two large tables were placed together and groups of from five to seven candidates were seated round them. The candidates were then told that they were required to hold discussions amongst themselves for a short period. They were to talk to one another and not address the observers, who would tap on the table with a pencil if they required the group's attention. Later on, they would be given specific questions and topics to discuss, but to begin with they were asked to find a topic for discussion. Candidates were told that they could smoke if they wished and the assessor usually ended his briefing with some such remark as: ". . . sex, religion, politics – nothing barred. Away you go!" At this stage interest centred upon who started the discussion, the topic or topics chosen, and whether or not they were developed by the whole group. Once this initial discussion was progressing in a reasonably lively manner, some of the following topics were introduced by one or other of the assessors. These topics were chosen to represent serious and humorous matters and to cover a fair range of subjects which, it was hoped, would bring out opinions held by candidates in as wide an area as possible. The list of topics and questions included:

(1) What is morale and how is it fostered?
(2) Are women the weaker sex?
(3) Is a third world war inevitable?
(4) We have had a Stone Age, Iron age, Bronze age, etc., which age comes next?
(5) It has been said that specialists in any field get to know more and more about less and less until they know everything about everything. Do you consider this to be a true statement?
(6) What are your views on race and colour bar?
(7) In choosing a job, what factors should a man consider?
(8) Does life end at 40?
(9) What is meant by "The Art of Living"?
(10) Is television a good thing?

Group Projects

The physical layout for the group projects was the same as for the group discussion with candidates sitting round a table. The projects used were of the short type which candidates were allowed 15 minutes to study. Discussions of the projects were allowed to run for about half an hour. In the briefing, candidates were told to use the first 15 minutes to familiarize themselves with the nature of the project and to make up their own minds about the issues involved. They were then told that as a group they were to discuss the various problems and come to the decisions indicated in the project. Projects were always read through by the assessors after a copy had been handed out to the candidates.

An Example of a Short Project

"The 'Consolidated Airline Co.' are sponsoring a series of sound radio broadcasts on civil aviation. One of these broadcasts will be a 30-minute programme on 'Civil Aviation from the Pilot's Viewpoint'.

"You as a group of pilots of the company have been brought together to discuss and plan this projected programme. The Chairman of the Company tells you that in this programme, as in the whole series of broadcasts, he is interested in telling the public just what problems civil aviation faces in this day and age. He is also interested in getting over to the general public the sort of work that is going on in civil aviation at present. The whole series of programmes are designed for the general public, who will probably not have any more technical knowledge than the average schoolboy.

"Taking into account the points mentioned above, you as a group are asked to discuss this project, particularly:

"(a) You are asked to make a decision as to what should be included in this programme and what aspects of the situation should be stressed.

"(b) You are asked to make some suggestions as to the actual layout of the programme.

"(c) You are asked to make some suggestions as to where in the whole series of broadcasts this one should come. Other topics to be covered in the series are: aircraft engineering and maintenance, planning schedules, commercial aspects, etc."

This form of project gives few facts to the discussion participants, which has the value of throwing them on to their own resources. Moreover, any candidate with "wild" ideas is given scope to present them. In this example, as in the other projects used, a civil aviation theme was used to guide the group discussion into task appropriate areas.

Chairmanship and Command Exercises

The first two exercises in the programme, which we have already discussed, were of the typical undirected or leaderless sort. For two reasons, however, it was felt that an exercise where each group member in turn was given charge of the discussion should be included. Firstly this was regarded as important in that it allowed us to see candidates operating in actual command. Secondly, by forcing a leading role on the quieter group member we see how they behave in a dynamic situation when officially given command. It could be levelled at leaderless discussions that the quick talker has an unfair advantage over his quieter colleague. This method of forcing each candidate into a leading role should overcome this.

The chairman, when his turn came, was given a 10-minute period in which he had to get the group to discuss the problems, and also in which he had to present a summary of findings or conclusions. Topics were again chosen for relevance to the job and designed so that the candidates' attitudes to certain aspects of the job would be reflected. In the following list of topics, problem 1, for example, would get at both the views held about pilots' status and also views on discipline.

Sample Problems for Chairmanship

(1) It has been the practice when night-stopping crews at Rome to accommodate all crew members in one first-class hotel. It has been decided that in future stewards and stewardesses will be housed in a different hotel of lower grade in the interests of discipline and economy.

(2) In the past promotion of pilots within the Company has been on merit. In future the policy will be to promote solely on seniority.

(3) It has been the practice in the past to allow crew members on night-stop to order early morning tea at the Comany's expense. In the interests of economy and to bring flying staff in line with ground staff, it has been decided that in future crews must pay for such amenities themselves.

(4) Because of increase in traffic the Company has found itself short of pilots. Therefore, pilots have been asked to give up part or all of their two weeks' summer leave and will be compensated by a bonus payment for each day given up.

Individual Situations

In these exercises, each candidate in turn was first asked to make a spot decision about a problem which had no one correct answer. Then in front of the group of candidates he was made to defend his choice of answer. His choice would be criticized and good reasons would be given why some better alternative solution might have been offered.

Strictly speaking, the individual situations exercise is not a group interview at all. It is included here merely to complete the picture, and also because it is an exercise often found in this type of group programme. In practice we found it to be useful only when it was already suspected of a certain candidate that he might crack under pressure. Here, in his response to an emotional problem, quite a lot of pressure could be brought to bear on him, his flexibility or rigidity thus assessed. As a general exercise, however, we found them to be undesirable. They broke up the group and forced the assessor himself to enter the situation. Furthermore, they introduced a note of fantasy contrary to the general spirit of pedestrian reality inherent in the procedure in general.

Individual Situation Examples

(1) You are staying in a hotel which catches fire. As you are escaping from your room you find you are in the position of being able to save one and only one of three people trapped in their respective rooms. One of these is a famous author and poet, the second a cripple child, and the third your cousin. Which one would you save?

(2) You are returning from a continental flight. You have been told that a lot of petty smuggling has been going on amongst crews and that you should be on the lookout for it. You are instructed to report afterwards to your Flight Manager. In the Customs shed you see a young stewardess, with whom you are very friendly, pushing some jewellery into the back of her handbag. A young trainee Customs Officer passes her luggage though you are sure he saw the jewellery. His Supervisor, who should have been present, was away at the time. What do you do?

Assessment of Candidates' Performance

Before the selection procedure was put into practice a series of discussions was held to consider what the qualities were which would give a young pilot command potential; in other words, what the leadership traits were for this situation. The first list obtained was further refined by giving a questionnaire to all senior pilots (Shouksmith, 1958). This produced a final list which can be seen in Table 8.2 and is the same as that given under the personality heading in the case study job analysis in Chapter 4. During the group sessions of the selection programme the observers had in front of them this list. Thus the observers had in mind throughout the group exercises a specific list of traits and would pay particular attention to any behaviour which would throw light on to the degree to which a candidate possessed any of these traits. During the actual interviews the observers used a sheet of foolscap paper with the

100   *Assessment through Interviewing*

TABLE 8.2. *List of command qualities used as traits on which candidates in pilot selection programme were rated*

Dependability	
Ability to inspire confidence	
Initiative	
Keenness	
Calmness	
Self-discipline	
Appearance and bearing	
Decisiveness	
Adaptability	
Co-operation	
Commands respect	
Sense of humour	
Breadth of outlook	

candidates' names in order of seating listed in the left-hand margin. On this sheet, alongside each candidate's name, the observer noted down significant points in that candidate's behaviour during the discussion. Table 8.3 shows an example, with fictitious candidates, of how these notes were made in practice.

At the end of the group sessions, the candidates were assessed for their degree of possession for each of the traits in Table 8.2, in terms of a five-point scale, A to E. The observers took each trait in turn and in terms of that trait rated the candidate as to whether he could be:

A. Strongly recommended.
B. Recommended.
C. A possible borderline.
D. Not recommended.
E. Definitely to be rejected.

From the rating on each individual trait a final overall rating for group exercises was given, in terms of the same five-point scale.

TABLE 8.3. *Notes taken during a discussion period on the candidates' participation*

(The notes given are a combination of notes made for the general discussion and for the project. They are combined in order to show the general value of the technique in one table.)

SMITH — Very self-assured, almost too much so — a little supercilious — undoubtedly able — keen sense of humour — argues by humorous anecdotes. Sense of responsibility might be low — narrow in approach though not in knowledge — logic not always clear. Conceited? Fades a little when faced with specific problem — would he fold under pressure?

JONES — Not really with the others — tends to commonplace arguments — rest of group seldom accept his points or arguments. Almost completely out of serious discussion on project — attempts to change topic about half-way through — unsuccessful.

BROWN — Some inferiority feelings? — a little immature. Leads group along but not always on point. Puts forward plenty of ideas but not always accepted. Pushed by others — stands up well under group pressure — attempts a summary — quite good.

ROBINSON — Says nothing for a long while — immaturity of expression — a good seconder but no leader — juvenile humour — rather facetious — regards project as beneath him — O.K. when drawn in by Grey.

GREY — Opens up on most topics — usually sensible — appears broader in outlook as discussion progresses — willing to accept others' views — approach is intellectual and good. Does most of actual planning of project and carries others along with him. Dry sense of humour. Smith arguing with him — now got it all his way. The one with the ideas and views accepted.

ARTHUR — Takes wider view — broad outlook but depth not lacking — quiet approach — rather hesitant about entering discussions — perhaps a little "weak-kneed". Logical approach to project — cannot grasp the lead.

Appraising the Procedure

I have suggested that to achieve adequate results in both the individual and the group interview three basic aspects must be controlled. These are, firstly, the background and planning of the interview, secondly, the orientation to the interview and the attitude of mind towards it which the interviewer has, and, finally, the method of conducting the interview. These aspects are controlled in slightly different ways for the two kinds of interview, but both should achieve the same results. The extent to which the scheme succeeded in practice can be seen in the Appendix, which describes a full analysis which was made of the procedure for selection of airline pilots outlined in this chapter.

It can be seen from this Appendix that each part of the procedure was playing a worth-while part in the end result. As far as the trait-rating method is concerned, this emerges as a highly reliable system. The overall figure for reliability of ratings on Command Potential between two assessors was 0.94. Although, as I have pointed out in the Appendix, this figure is probably an inflated estimate, since common training of assessors and the intergroup nature of the ratings would tend to increase it, it is nevertheless sufficiently high to suggest that the technique is basically sound. Personal bias has been kept to a minimum it would seem – unless it is assumed that the four assessors concerned had identical biases. The trait-rating method, operating as the group interview counterpart of the "critical requirements" of the individual interview, is also seen to produce the reliability required.

Finally, it can be seen that the procedure as a whole was worth while. Wastage rate during training and the first 6 months "on the line" was reduced from something of the order of 12% to about 4%. Ratings made by the Flight Managers of the Corporation showed that not only was the general standard of new recruits high, but that there was a substantial measure of agreement between the Flight Managers' assessment of the new pilots' "Command Potential" after two years in the Corporation and the assessment made by the Final Selection Board after seeing them as candidates for 2 days. In general, it can be concluded that what was suggested theoretically as being sound, did in fact work out in practice.

PART III

Interviews, Groups, and Social Behaviour

CHAPTER 9

The Interview and Group Theory

In a basic interview two people come together and engage in conversation; the group interview consists of the same process except that more than two people are involved. In each situation the participants interact verbally for some particular and specific purpose. We can regard the interview as constituting what Cooley (1909) calls a "primary group", that is a group where members are in direct association one with another in face-to-face relationships. Through the years both psychologists and sociologists have been concerned to investigate the nature of groups and their functioning and have arrived at coalescing views about the ways in which groups operate. Since both group selection procedures and individual interviews may be regarded as primary groups, we should be able to gain a better understanding of how they operate by analysing them in terms of small group theory.

The interview, I have said, is an interaction process. The simplest possible interaction is when A speaks to B and B receives the message. This is one-way interaction, but the true interaction of the interview is a two-way process, where A speaks to B, B receives the message and replies. When a whole series of these interactions take place we have what may be regarded as a "social episode", the interview being one example of a social episode. Thus in studying what happens in the interview we are concerned with studying the interaction process, the way in which such a series of interactions takes place. In the individual interview, which is a special form of the dyad or two-person group, the two participants each come to it with their own particular repertoire of behaviour patterns and combinations of behaviour patterns. Any given person has limits to the sort of behaviour he or she can produce, limits which are imposed by the kind of person he or she is. I behave as I do because I have learned, through past experience, to behave in a certain way. This is so for everyone, and the way in which any individual behaves is a reflection of the kind of person he or she is, of the personality each has. In the verbal interaction process which is the interview, how the person talks, what he talks about, and the attitudes he reveals towards various subjects throws light on his personality. But there are two people in an interview and in the conversation which follows their coming together, ideas are exchanged, views are sought and given, and what is revealed by the candidate, his participation in the social episode, depends not only on his own repertoire of behaviour but also on the behaviour repertoire of the other member of the dyad, the interviewer. At any one moment, interaction can be described in terms of the two patterns of behaviour which A and B are enacting and theoretically the interview can include all possible combinations of all A's behaviour items and all B's behaviour items. Each is an individual; each has his own personality, character, and temperament; each has developed habitual ways of reacting in the presence of others. There can, theoretically, be many combinations of interactions between them, the limits being set only by their individual behaviour repertoires. In practice, one particular pattern of interaction develops out of all the possible interactions which could develop out of the two participants' repertoires. Why a particular pattern develops on a given occasion is the essential question in analysing interviewing.

This approach to the study of dyads, though not specifically interviews, has been given a conceptual framework by Thibaut and Kelley (1959) in their theory of group functioning. Thibaut and Kelley's theory uses as its base Homans' (1958) sociological concept of social behaviour being an exchange process with reward and cost elements. The behavioural outcomes of this exchange or interaction process are seen to depend on each individual's position regarding a number of group-derived or group-related factors. Among the most important of these group-derived or related factors are, firstly, the set of *attitudes* brought to the group by all its members, secondly, the prescriptions for behaviour which emerge from the interplay of attitudes — known as the *norms* of behaviour for the group — and, thirdly, the expectancies which define *roles* for group members and which are usually developed from the group norms. A fourth important determinant of group behaviour is, of course, the task set the group or goal towards which it is striving. All of these together, we may presume, influence each individual, so feeding back on to the attitude-set associated with the group, possibly modifying each individual's attitudes and so sowing the seed for group development.

Thibaut and Kelley's approach exemplifies the communality of approach between psychologist and sociologist in this area. A second theory, that of Mills (1964), starting from a sociological viewpoint, also arrives at similar conclusions though emphasizing different facets. Mills bases his analysis on a modified interaction measurement procedure called Sign Process Analysis. From the results of action analyses of groups, using this procedure, he isolates a number of variables which are seen to influence interaction of and in the group. The variables Mills isolates are similar to those used by Thibaut and Kelley, which makes the two analyses mutually supportive. Mills, however, follows sociological tradition and emphasizes the early development of roles in the life cycle of a group. A normative system, he suggests, develops once group roles have been modelled. If we put together the two sets of ideas embodied in these two theories, we find that the differences which emerge are of minor nature only, and produced in the main by the psychological emphasis in one on the individual and the sociological emphasis on the group in the other. By implanting Thibaut and Kelley's individual focus into Mills' concept of the developmental cycle of a group we can produce a general schema of group action (as seen in Table 9.1) which will act as a framework for understanding both group and individual interviews.

The four basic components influencing individuals within a group are thus seen to be: attitudes, norms, roles and tasks or goals. The attitudes you have towards a situation will obviously affect your reaction to it or behaviour in that situation. "Norms", which one can define as the prescribed behaviour for a given society or group since they *are* prescriptions for behaviour, should control it to some extent. We all regard certain ways of behaving as acceptable and others as not.

TABLE 9.1 *The life cycle of a group*

A group follows a "life cycle" in a number of sequential phases. Sometimes the phases overlap, however, and the sequence is only roughly followed.

Phase 1. *The encounter:* Where group members get to know one another and test the boundaries of possible interaction for this group.

Phase 2. (a) *Norm development:* In preliminary interchanges, members gradually reveal and exchange attitudes. Through the interplay of attitudes, certain prescriptions for behaviour in this group emerge and develop. These formalized prescriptions for behaviour specifying accepted and precluded behaviour patterns are the group's indigenous normative system.

(b) The normative system provides expectancies for behaviour, and members fit their own behaviour patterns to these, so developing specific group roles.

Phase 3. *Production and Development*
(a) Task-oriented behaviour occurs to make the group productive and move it towards its goals.

(b) As general behaviour occurs within the group and *role relationships* are established, individual attitudes and behaviours become modified.

Phase 4. *Separation or Change:* As goals are reached and attitudes modified, the group ends its primary life cycle. Then, either the members separate or the group alters its norms, roles, and role relationships to orient itself towards new and modified goals.

Furthermore, what is acceptable in one situation might not be in another; what can be done and is the "norm" for behaviour in a dance hall would not be acceptable in a church. Since the norms for a given situation define what is acceptable, right, and proper for that situation, they will control the interaction to some extent. On the other hand, they do not operate in the same way as attitudes. A person's attitude to a particular situation will control his behaviour in that situation. There is, however, nothing to stop anyone behaving contrary to the norm and, indeed, there are many individuals who delight in behaving contrary to the proper and normal fashion.

Probably "norms" operate more through setting up expectancies rather than directly. A candidate coming to be interviewed for a technical job will expect to be asked about his technical proficiency and will act accordingly. He will take a certain "role", at the outset of the interview at least, a role based on his expectancies. The interviewer himself, if he follows the "Hawthorne rules for conduct" of the interview, will have certain norms and these will dictate the role he takes in the interview, the role of listener who merely stimulates conversation. Finally, the task the interviewer is set, the goal which has to be reached, channels the discussion into a particular direction and so is responsible in major part for the limiting of all possible interactions to the eventuating few.

This conceptualization of the dyad when applied specifically to the interview is very similar to an earlier one made by Allport (1937), who suggested that interviewing involves three factors which are also common to other judgement situations. Firstly, there is the skill of the interviewer. Secondly, there is what Allport refers to as the "openness or enigmatic quality of the subject himself", and, finally, the selection and framing of the questions that will reveal significant and trustworthy information concerning the subject is also deemed to be important. The second of these, the "openness or enigmatic quality of the subject", relates to the attitudes, values, etc., which the subject has, since they make him what he is and also dictate the role he plays. The skill of the interviewer is represented by his role in the interaction process and depends in part on his attitudes and also, as we have seen, on his orientation to the task in hand in terms of the Hawthorne rules. Again, the final point of Allport's — in terms of this analysis — relates to the task. What the interviewer is set to assess will dictate which topics he will want to cover, which questions he will ask. This is where the "critical requirements" are important; they direct the interviewer on to particular areas and constitute the "task" for the interview.

Whilst not making such a complete analysis of all the factors, other authors have reached similar conclusions about the concepts which are important in interviewing. Oldfield (1941), for example, stresses the importance of attitudes and speaks of the interview as a means by which the candidate is brought to display his attitudes and in its cognitive aspects a means whereby these attitudes may be perceived. Sarbin (1954) makes "role" the central concept in describing interactions between two people. A role is defined as a sequence of learned actions performed by a person in an interaction situation. Within the interaction situation, Sarbin suggests that each person takes a role in response to his perception of the other, the latter confirming or correcting his initial expectancies. One can conclude that a role is in part based on attitudes, since Sarbin speaks of learned patterns, and also of basing actions on one's perceptions of the other member of the dyad, and, as Oldfield points out, such perceptions are concerned with attitudes. Moreover, Sarbin refers later on to the particular role which appears, depending not only on the anticipated behaviour but also on the behaviour which it is desired to produce. This, it seems to me, refers to a motivating factor which channels in the interview situation the conversation and also the roles adopted.

Summing up what has been said so far, it does seem that there is sufficient agreement to suggest that concepts like "attitudes", "roles", "norms", "expectancies", "tasks", etc., can be usefully applied to an analysis of interviewing. Just how they operate and to what extent they are of equal or varying importance, remains undemonstrated. Thus, in an attempt to throw some light on the situation, I carried out a small experiment on the effect of different instructions on the interview situation. Forty-eight students from two under-graduate applied psychology classes were placed in pairs and given the following quotation from H. W. Van Loon (Hepner, 1951) to study:

> "The purpose of education is to get a perspective of yourself so that you can understand yourself in relation to those around you. This enables you to live an active and pleasant life. It enables you to go through the world with the least amount of friction and a proper amount of understanding. This is all that education is supposed to do. . . .
>
> "Let's look at our schools and see what is going on. We find that they are doing little in the way of educating students. The schools are simply big play pens where the incompetent can send their children."

There were two sets of instructions available, one member of each pair being given instructions A, the other member instructions B. These instructions defined the roles which each member of the pair should take in the following interaction.

INSTRUCTIONS FOR PERSON A

"Attempt to find the attitude to this statement of your partner. Does he (she) agree or disagree? Does he (she) make a good case out for his (her) beliefs?"

INSTRUCTIONS FOR PERSON B

"Make up your own mind on this statement — particularly as to whether you agree or disagree with the general conclusion. Put your point of view to your partner and if necessary attempt to persuade him or her."

Readers will see that these instructions virtually give to A the role of an assessment interviewer and in a sense B's role fits in

with this. In fact, since it was first used for experimental purposes, I have used this situation in training courses as a basis for discussion about roles in the interview. In the initial experimental use of the situation, each pair was given periods of 15 — 30 minutes in which to discuss the statement in line with their briefings. Each pair was then asked how far they had succeeded in the role for which they had been briefed and were asked their general feelings about the whole situation. From their comments, three major findings emerged:

(1) None of those taking role A were fully persuaded of their partner's point of view. Seven, however, reported that they found their partner's arguments convincing.

(2) The majority of the As, twenty out of twenty-four, stated that they were unable to get a clear picture of what B's arguments for a particular point of view were.

(3) Eighteen out of the twenty-four taking role B reported that as a result of the interaction they altered their views.

When one observed the various pairs during the course of discussion it was noticeable that the role ascribed to people not only defined the content of their conversation but also their manner of conduct. Those taking role B, without exception, tended to take a very definite line, in some cases amounting to belligerance. Persons taking role A, on the other hand, tended to give little away, to question much, and to adopt a "not-convinced" attitude. They had probably been reading about non-directive counselling which would account for their non-committal attitude. The effect of this approach was often to make person B become rather desperately aggressive towards the end of the discussion, as if he were worried at being unable to get anywhere with his opponent. Against this background the significant finding that eighteen of the role B students changed or altered their own views during discussion is extremely interesting. At least it suggests that the calm, inquiring manner of role A made B re-think. It might also suggest that this non-directive, questioning approach has potent hidden powers for persuasion.

Since making the original study, further data with different subjects and different tasks has indicated that situational variables, the task set, and the norms for the indigenous group from which the subjects came, may all influence the outcome of the interaction.† In a group of hospital ward sisters, for example, discussant B proved to be less likely to change her mind; she remained authoritatively dominant in the interaction situation. In this case the "norms" of the occupational group from which the participants came and the background situation, not being connected with a psychology class concerned with interviewing, seemed to change the result. The finding indicates that in assessment interviews, particularly the group interview which is not directed from within, the norms of behaviour brought to the group by participants from their own social groups will be reflected in their behaviour in the assessment group.

Reverting to the general findings, we note that conclusion 1 suggests that the role set person A also prevented him from being persuaded by person B. In the interview situation this would be equivalent to the interviewer keeping an open mind and assessing the candidate's attitudes without being influenced by them or necessarily identifying with them. This is important if prejudice and bias are to be kept to a minimum and would seem possible if the correct role is followed. The instructions gave person A an orientation in the same way as the Hawthorne rules do the interviewer; the conclusion is that the interviewer's orientation, or attitudes, control the role he takes, and it is this role which determines the course the interaction takes.

Though attitudes account for a large part of the variance of a given interview, for the direction the interaction process takes, the specific task of assessment in a given situation must also be important. Allport (1937), referring to the third of the factors he mentions as being involved in the interview, adds a very

†I am grateful to Nan Kinross and her staff in the Nursing Studies Unit, Department of Psychology, Massey University, for providing data on this topic.

important rider. His third factor concerns the framing of appropriate questions to reveal significant and trustworthy information regarding the subject, and in doing this he points out that one must first know what the goal of the interview is. In the experimental situation, the majority of the As found it difficult to obtain a clear picture of B's opinions. This in part was no doubt due to the fact that B was allowed to take a dominant role which diverged from that of A, a situation which would not exist in the assessment interview. More important, however, is the fact that A's task was not specific enough. In Chapter 2 I pointed out that "Unless the interviewer knows exactly what he is looking for, the interaction becomes undirected, the conversation without purpose, and thus, one might argue, no longer truly an interview." This conclusion, based on reported evidence of reliability and validity studies of the interview, stresses the importance of the "task" which is set for a particular interview situation. The critical requirements, or specific assessment task, set the limits to the areas for discussion in the interaction process; they constitute the equivalent of the "goal" which Allport suggests controls the interview's course; they are a second set of variables, along with attitudes, which specify the interviewer's role.

In summary, when we analyse the interview as a social episode we find that what dictates the course of the interaction is the role of the interviewer. The interviewer's role, the pattern of activity he emits in the interview, is dependent on two things. Firstly, it depends on his attitudes, not only his general attitudes to life and about life but more particularly the particular set of attitudes he has towards interviewing. Thus if he follows and accepts the programme for interviewing which I have put forward in this book, he will have certain attitudes about interviewing, a certain orientation to it, and these factors will determine the role he will take. But this is not all. His role will be further defined by the "task", specific to a certain assessment situation, which he is set. The "critical requirements" which he must assess further modify his role, leading his pattern of activity into certain channels, further restricting it from his total behaviour reservoir.

The candidate, on the other hand, comes to the interview with certain expectancies, it is true. These may determine his approach and orientation to the interview itself, but once the interview has begun he will modify his role to fit the wants and demands of the interviewer. Most candidates want to impress the interviewer, so that the motivating factors which Sarbin (1954) mentions are mostly concerned with following the pattern of actions desired by the interviewer. In the free-flowing interviewing advocated here, the expectancies of candidates are often confounded, and the candidate finds himself or herself taking a role far different from the one they anticipated. As one girl interviewed in the N.A.C. flight reservations clerk programme put it: "I don't feel as though I've been interviewed at all. We've just had a friendly chat!"

In the practical situation, for the interview to be successful, the interviewer must first understand fully its specific purpose. This will dictate the role which he must take in order to direct the conversation towards that purpose. The role of the interviewer, also based on his attitudes which are expressed in his orientation to the interview, is of basic importance. Since the tone of the interview — its pace, level, and manner — all depend on the interviewer, who controls the interaction in a dyad whose purpose is some specific assessment, the candidate's role — though not his level of participation — must be subservient. As a general rule my experience of interviewing has led me to conclude that most value is gained from an interview where the interviewer takes a "non-directive, reflective" role; one in which the interviewer follows the Hawthorne rules against a biographical setting. If the interviewer has a firm explicit purpose in mind he can, without being overforceful, still control the interview and any attitudes about assessment which the candidate has will not affect the course of interaction — unless the interviewer wishes them to do so. It is the interviewer's attitudes allied to a specific purpose which direct his, the controlling role, and so determine the course of the interview.

We have already noted certain essential differences between group and individual interviews notably in the way that the specific purpose is met by pre-setting the task for the group and in the assessor for a group interview not being a participant. Findings from practical applications of group assessment exercises, as shown in the Appendix, indicate that assessments from them do differ from those obtained from individual interviews. Again the theory can account for this. Not only is the task internal to the group, thereby affecting the norms and roles for the group, but initial participation is based on different instructions so that it takes a different form. What remains as the important concept which explains the interaction process in both group and individual interview is that of "attitude". In the group exercise the candidates' attitudes to the assessment situation in general, to group interaction, to the other candidates, and to the particular problem which is posed, will control their contributions to the social episode. Their attitudes, together with the problem posed, will control the roles they take. Thus the problem takes the place of the individual interviewer's task, the difference in the individual interview being that there the interviewer's attitudes and his task give him a certain controlling role. In this controlled interaction the candidate cannot possibly display leadership. In the group situation the problem operates directly as a controlling influence and not through one member of the group. Thus any candidate who through having the correct attitudes can achieve a controlling role for any part of the interaction process is displaying successful leadership.

CHAPTER 10

Beyond Assessment

This book has been concerned with assessment interviewing as it is used in the selection of staff. This, as I stressed at the outset, is only one kind of interviewing; there are many other varieties. In what I hope has been a basic primer, it is not unnatural that I have stressed selection interviewing which *is* the basic type. There were selection interviews long before there was a study of psychology. In all probability the first time one man employed another the interview was born. As we have seen, this simplest form of interviewing is fraught with many difficulties, so it would be a very unwise man who went beyond assessment before he had fully mastered the basic principles.

Even assessment interviewing when used in situations other than that required to select one or more candidates for a specific job, looses its basic simplicity. The initial interview in a vocational guidance situation, for example, although it is in a way still concerned with assessment, adds problems for the interviewer. Whereas in selection work the interviewer has a list of critical requirements directing his attention to certain limited areas, in the case of a vocational guidance interview he has to find out what are the critical factors in the person who has come for guidance. When a person comes for help in choosing a suitable career the first step which the guidance worker has to take is to assess just what the interests, personality characteristics, and strong and weak points of the individual are. It would be a Herculean and impossible task for the interviewer to give a complete picture of the interviewee. By following the general biographical method and probing in particular the interviewee's interests, hobbies, pastimes and skills, future hopes and past achievements, he can gain some insight into the essential areas for occupational choice.

But vocational guidance, by its very name, suggests something more than this widened form of assessment. Once the critical aspects for career choice have been assessed, the interviewer's next task is to match these with specific and possible jobs. The vocational guidance worker needs to have available classified information about jobs so that he can match individuals with possible careers. He must be able to give the interviewee information about occupations and help him come to some decision. Sometimes the client can work things out for himself but at others, as Hoppock (1957) puts it:". . . the client needs help to get the essential information to appraise its accuracy, or to see how it relates to his problem, or . . . in considering his own reaction to the information."

Now we have gone beyond assessment; we are speaking of interviews where the process of interaction is used in order to help or assist someone in the widest sense, where the interview is used for therapeutic purposes.

Therapeutic psychology is a term used by Brammer and Shostrom (1960) to refer to a number of related professions all of which are concerned with helping people in some way or other. In the same sense we can talk about therapeutic interviewing when the chief aim of the interview is not to assess someone's potential but to help them in some way or another. All of us meet various mental and emotional problems in our life, though most of the time we manage to cope with them adequately. Occasionally, however, a problem arises which is too difficult. It may be something minor, such as a difficulty in studying at school or college, something more serious, e.g. an inability to adjust to the problems and demands of marriage, or a serious shock which leads to a complete emotional breakdown. In any of these circumstances we should require help, although the help required would be rather different in each case. Obviously the assistance appropriate to a schoolboy who has to choose a career for himself is vastly different from the help required by someone who has suffered an emotional disturbance or nervous breakdown. Therapeutic interviewing is, in fact, merely a convenient title covering a number of different techniques and methods.

The manner in which help can best be given depends in part on the nature of the problem presented by the individual seeking help. In all therapeutic interviews, however, the general purpose becomes attitude or personality change rather than attitude or personality assessment. The specific purpose will still vary and consequently vary the nature of the interview according to the behaviour problem or emotional maladjustment with which the client requires help. The disturbed, even neurotic person, as I have pointed out previously (Shouksmith, 1960a), is still sufficiently in contact with the real world to take an active and productive part in his own therapy. More seriously disturbed people, whom we may refer to as psychotics, find that life is so intolerable that they have, as it were, withdrawn from the world. They have lost contact with reality and so cannot interact, in therapy, in the same way as those with minor disturbances. For the normal, the neurotic, or the psychotic, problems which constitute a bar to adjustment may arise in any one of many areas which affect the civilized and socialized human being. In the past, writers have distinguished clearly between varieties of helping related to types of problems. Hahn and MacLean (1955), for example, distinguish between "guidance" as dealing with more or less practical matters of courses to be taken to solve a particular problem, and "counselling" where the interviewer's task is to help the client or patient to learn afresh and gain new perceptions and insights of himself and his problems. At more intensive levels of "help", Brammer and Shostrom speak, on the one hand, of counselling which emphasizes re-education and situational problem solving, where the supportive effect of the counsellor is minimal and psychotherapy, on the other hand, where the interview focuses on the unconscious, attempting to reconstruct the patient's behaviour often through depth analysis. Modern research into the helping function (Carkhuff, 1969) suggests that essentially the process remains the same, even if the task differs, a conclusion which fits the general conception of interviewing presented here. A better classification might well be made in terms of the degree of structure introduced into the helping process (Brammer, 1973) with "the formality of the professional helping process" being distinguished from the relatively informal, haphazard and unstructured acts of helping associated with friends, family, and general community endeavours. As Brammer also points out, the helper is also a person, with thoughts and feelings, and so a guiding theory of helping assists the therapist in focusing on the client's problems. If the counsellor "is going to work systematically in a helping function", Brammer argues, "he needs some 'hooks' on which to hang his experiences and some frame of reference for gaining perspectives on his work and improving his services". This theory need not necessarily be one concerned with the essential nature of human personality, as earlier bases for psychodynamic therapy were, but may simply be an understanding of the interaction—interview process. From research and practice we have found that behaviour and attitudes will both be revealed and modified most readily in a free interaction where the interviewer is accepting and has empathy for the problems of the client. The interviewer's task, or specific purpose, is to isolate the client's problems, clarify and untangle them, and help him come to terms with them and solve them. To the assessment approach to interviewing one component is added. This is "feedback", which adds the control element to interpersonal communications processes (Burgoon *et al.*, 1974). Feedback implies using what the client says to give an understanding of his problems. The counsellor or helper first elicits information from the client about his thoughts and feelings in key areas, related to problem issues. Then he feeds back to the client what he has obtained, so that the client can see it himself in a new light and judge its meaningfulness for and impact on him as a person. The manner in which feedback is given will no doubt vary from counsellor to counsellor. A psychodynamic therapist will interpret the findings in terms of the psychodynamic model of behaviour he operates from then report back to his client what everything "means" in terms of that theory. The non-directive therapist will simply wish to paraphrase or reflect the words of his client in ways which focus on the problem from which the client can make his own decisions. Without knowledge of his own behaviour and its nature in relation to the context in which it is emitted, a client is unlikely to improve. "Oh that some power the gift to gie us, to see ourselves as others see us." But not all feedback is helpful. To be helpful it must not be threatening to the client and his stability or else he will fail to use it. Such non-threatening and helpful feedback, Johnson (1972) believes, must have certain characteristics and not others. As summarized below, feedback in interpersonal behaviour concentrates on those aspects itemized in the left-hand column of Table 10.1.

TABLE 10.1. *Characteristics of helpful feedback in interpersonal situations*

Feedback is helpful if it focuses on:	Feedback is not helpful if it emphasises:
Behaviour	Abstract qualities of the individual
Observations	Inferences
Descriptions	Judgements
Discussion and sharing of ideas and information	Giving advice
Exploring alternative approaches to problems.	Answers and solutions

Counselling in Practice

The popular conception of therapy is probably someone "giving advice" to someone else. This idea is akin to the old idea of how an assessment interview should be carried on, and, as we have seen in modern conceptions, both fields are vastly different. In fact the free, easy method working in terms of the Hawthorne rules seems closely akin to modern counselling techniques. It is neither possible nor appropriate for me in a book of this nature to attempt to give a detailed account of various counselling techniques of which there are probably as many as there are counsellors. The reader who wishes to pursue this matter further can do so through any of the entirely adequate standard texts (Brammer, 1973; Arbuckle, 1961; Rogers, 1942). Essentially counselling refers to an interaction process where the major emphasis is on problem solving. In the dyad one member acts in the supportive role of "organizing learning situations in such a manner that his client will, after gaining new perceptions and insight into his problem, change his behaviour from what it was to something more personally satisfying and socially acceptable" (Hahn and MacLean, 1955). To achieve this the counsellor must have certain attitudes and take a certain role. The exact attitudes and role will depend on his theoretical outlook. In this, as in all human endeavours, fashions vary, and what is popular at one time will be "out" at some other period. Currently, many counsellors adopt a permissive, client-centred, problem-solving attitude. They are prepared to accept the client as he is with all his quirks and foibles and they own that they are not an outside authority applying skills to help a person. It is out of the relationship itself, the interaction process, that development occurs.

These attitudes lead the counsellor to take a role in the interview which is generally reflective and only secondarily interpretive. This conception allows for the presentation of information to the client, which in the course of interaction is assimilated by him and for the clarification of issues or structuring of problem situations through discussion. Hence it offers a reasonably comprehensive framework for the counsellor's role. The chief ingredients of this role, however, for most counsellors appears to be firstly reflecting problems and difficulties and restructuring them. We are, in all therapeutic interviews, concerned with attitude change. The counsellor who attempts to achieve this through reflection attempts to express through new words the essential attitudes which the client reveals, so that in seeing them in new lights, he understands them better and perhaps learns to overcome them.

As the process of counselling continues, the interviewer may gradually modify his role so that as well as reflecting he is also "clarifying issues", throwing new light on problems. This, of course, will not be successful until he has been accepted by the client as a satisfactory counsellor or until the relationship is well established. Sometimes interpretation may also be introduced, though this depends on the outlook of the counsellor. Some counsellors will argue that it is only permissible to move beyond reflection to the clarification of implicitly arrived at assumptions which the client has. It would seem to me that to move beyond this to the discussion of issues which may be a little beyond the client's awareness even, is still useful provided any interpretation made is in terms of the candidate's own awareness and experience and not made through some abstract theory. Furthermore, there must be no attempt to thrust an interpretation on the client without allowing argument. Interpretation should be a basis of discussion and relearning and not an end in itself.

When the problem behaviour becomes such that the person involved tends to lose contact with reality so that he or she can no longer take a very active role in helping themselves, then deeper counselling, which is often referred to as psychotherapy, is required. Some psychologists feel that no interpersonal approach will succeed with such patients (Eysenck, 1952) and argue for direct behaviour modification using learning theory based on manipulations of the patient's behaviour by selectively rewarding desired behaviours. When a psychotherapeutic approach is taken to this seriously maladjusted group of patients, the emphasis is no longer on corporate problem solving but rather on the therapist giving a focused support to the patient. The therapist takes on the patient and his troubles and analyses and reconstructs his behaviour problems. Thus the role of the psychotherapeutic interviewer is one of undisguised analysis and interpretation. The psychotherapist normally has a conception of personality which must be sufficiently all-embracing to give an explanation of all the behaviour problems, each with its own varied background, that he meets with in his patients. The psychotherapist delves into his patient's unconscious to find the causes of problems. He may confront the patient with reasons for implicitly held beliefs and will endeavour to reach the ultimate roots of the patient's problems which may be in the forgotten depths of his unconscious. Once these root causes are found, the therapist will suggest and implant in his patient's mind ideas for new growth patterns which will, if followed, lead the patient to better and more mature adjustments.

Appraisal Interviewing in Business and Industry

In industrial and commercial settings, the annual evaluation of staff usually calls for an interview of the staff member being appraised or evaluated, this interview being carried out by some senior supervisor or manager. These annual interviews used to be regarded as assessment situations. More recently, however, the tendency has been to regard them as being exercises in staff development, where, through the interview, the employee and his supervisor review the preceding year, look at the problems which have arisen, and try to work out better behavioural approaches and procedures for the year to come. In this way the interview becomes both a decision-making dyadic group and a "helping" interview for the subordinate, encouraging him to better personal development. Maier (1958) has discussed the effectiveness of different approaches to the appraisal interview and concludes that a typical "counselling" approach is more effective than the older style evaluation exercise. Maier contrasts three approaches, the "tells", the "sells", and the problem-solving approach. In the first two of these the typical evaluation exercise consists of rating the employee and then "telling" him what his faults are and giving him a course of action for improvement or "selling" him what he ought to do to meet his supervisor's requirements for him. In the problem-solving approach both the appraisor and appraisee are seen to have a problem if things are not going well, and the appraisal interview becomes a mutual problem-solving exercise with no evaluation being made or blame attached. This latter approach fits well with modern conceptions of management by objectives, O.D., or participative management. Group interviewing also has its very real place in this field. Many industries now call conferences to discuss production, staffing, or other problems, and these are nothing less than group dynamic sessions. Since Hawthorne days it has been abundantly clear that counselling of employees individually can lead to better job satisfaction and higher productivity, so the role of counsellor in the occupational world is well established. As Bellows (1961) puts it, however: "The counsellor in industry who is to be concerned primarily with adjustment of workers and with therapeutic counselling probably should be a trained clinical psychologist." It is easy to talk about counselling but far more difficult to practise it. The wise personnel or administrative officer thinks twice before venturing beyond assessment.

CHAPTER 11

Groups as Forces for Change

The assessment group interview is one example of the small, primary social group in action. It is, like all groups, a dynamic entity within which counteracting forces, the tensions within individual participants which they bring to the group and the tensions produced within the group through the need to direct efforts towards the common task — battle for supremacy. These various tensions and driving forces influence the group, temporarily or lastingly, and become accepted or rejected by the group as bases for action. Through perceiving these forces, thinking and "feeling" about them, recalling relevant and related past experiences and acting out solutions, the group finds means by which these tensions can be reduced, problems solved, and goals achieved. This process involves change which is a learning process through which cognitive structures requiring new knowledge, motivational changes involving the learning of new likes and dislikes, the accepting of new values, and changes in group feelings of belongingness, are all actualized. Through the group new behaviours are made more readily available and individuals learn new attitudes, new values and new norms of interpersonal behaviour. The basic theory underlying this conception of groups as change agents can be traced to the work of Lewin (1947). Lewin also showed that these ideas could be used to foster planned change, showing that certain methods of group discussion were superior to more formal techniques, and to individual instruction in changing ideas and social behaviour. So was devised the idea of using dynamic groups, discussion groups, or group interviews as agents for change in the development of individuals' attitudes and personalities or in the development of complete and complex organizations. Encounter groups, sensitivity training, T-groups, and group psychotherapy are all variations of this new approach to using group processes to foster social and individual change.

Action Research

In the assessment group interview the interaction process is used by the observers for accumulating data about the participants. The interview may also be extended in its use as a research tool by using the group to investigate itself. In a recent management development programme I have used this approach, involving senior managers in participative group sessions whose task was to isolate factors enhancing and detracting from the growth of the company in which they were employed. The value of this type of research, however, is, as Lewin pointed out, that in looking at themselves and their problems such groups not only arrive at solutions but in the process of researching the problem the members of the group develop better human relationships and change attitudes and behaviour so that many of the problems disappear. The Hawthorne investigations discovered many years ago that intervention to find the problems often also coincidentally produced results. This is the basis of "action research" where any theoretical analysis becomes subsidiary to practical considerations of achieving some required group or organizational change. There are signs of growth already in the group mentioned above.

Action research programmes can be extensive as well as intensive and still be effective. In another major programme I used the supervisors themselves, allocated to 8- to 12-man groups, to investigate supervisory training needs amongst 200+ supervisors in the fibres division of a large international organization. In three group sessions, supervisors discussed amongst themselves and with myself and my colleagues involved in the project, the problems of supervisors and their specific training needs. Not only were specific factors requiring change isolated, but the joint resources of the supervisory groups, working through the interaction process, provided solutions for many of the problems. The group interviews used to isolate the problems became learning sessions for the participants. Problems affecting a particular participating supervisor were distinguished from those concerning and involving the whole group. The solutions for individual problems were often to be found in the group and the participants with these problems developed solutions for themselves through the interaction. Some major problems were identified and passed on to senior management as requiring formal training or organizational change for their solution. The same group approach was used with top management in formulating appropriate organizational changes to meet the revealed needs. In this way analysis and growth occurred together through the medium of group interaction.

Group Psychotherapy

The group interview is used as a formal method for fostering personal growth and development in psychotherapy. Group psychotherapy is based on the same principle as that on which action research is based, but formulated with a different focus. The basis for group psychotherapy rests, as Walton (1971) indicates, on the finding that "the way in which the group affected the behaviour of the individual not only cast a light on his personality, but was also capable of influencing it profoundly". The beginnings of group psychotherapy were also grounded in Freudian psychodynamics, which provided the group and the group therapist with a theoretical basis for interpreting behaviour in the group. The personality of the adult involved in therapy is seen as one structured by a range of dynamic systems relating to one another and objects in the person's world. In the individual in need of therapy these dynamic systems are seen to be imbalanced and unintegrated. The aim of group psychotherapy is to enable the patient to experience, in relation to others, the nature of his segregated systems, so that he can build them together under the control of the central adaptive power of the ego or self-concept. The learning process involves the patient having his thoughts and feelings interpreted so that he can understand them more clearly, understand how the motivating and directing systems in his personality have upset the balance of relationships in his inner world. The therapist becomes the focus for the group, and common worries and themes emerge, are exposed to the group, dealt with, and new relationships suggested and tried out. In this process the role of the therapist is obviously of supreme importance. In this respect the therapeutic group interview differs from the assessment one. The therapist takes part in, and indeed is said to control the interaction, and his style is all important in determining the therapeutic outcome. Walton (1971) argues that in general the conductor of group therapy should be non-didactic, permissive, and directive only in so far as he encourages group members through uncensored verbal communications to reveal their thoughts and experiences in the group as freely as they can. As decisions are made and changes take place in the group, the controller ensures that all members are aware of these and their significance both to the group and to its several members. As the therapy progresses he intervenes in the interaction only to clarify, summarize, and generalize; eventually, he decides when the members are ready to stand alone and so decides and moves the group towards a termination date which is mutually advantageous to all group members.

T-Groups and Human Relations Training

The emphasis in group psychotherapy is on the controller of the sessions and his leadership role. In contrast to this the most modern developments in group experiences aimed at personal development and change, stress the developmental or power for teaching of the group itself. The idea owes its origins, according to Smith (1973), to a group of psychologists working at the Massachusetts Institute of Technology who were running a two-week workshop for leaders of local Connecticut communities aimed at reducing tensions in these communities. Some of the course members overheard staff members discussing recorded tapes of the group sessions and found this a highly valuable experience. From this experience it was a small step to the basic T-group idea in which participants discuss themselves and the way they see themselves relating to one another in a small, unstructured, face-to-face group — or "group interview". Varieties of this basic experience have been developed under names like "T-groups", "sensitivity training", "laboratory training" or "encounter groups". They share certain characteristics, in their generally unplanned nature, the role of the leader or "facilitator" which is never forcefully directive of the group's activities, and their stress on "emotional" personal learning rather than intellectual learning, the "here and now" development rather than the problems of the past. The use of this kind of group experience in an integrated learning programme produces what has become called human relations training. Special exercises are used which direct the attention of the group to desired change areas, usually aiming at personal development or a change in attitude of group members. Human relations training has been applied to educational problems, community involvement programmes, motivation of industrial supervisors, and various facets of personal development. It is an exciting new use for the old group interview.

A Warning

In the T-group field there are many enthusiasts. One problem with enthusiasts is that all too often they accept the object of their enthusiasm without criticism or objective evaluation. Among T-group users, there are those whose use of the technique is based on too little knowledge and too loose a control of the human factors and emotions involved. T-groups grew out of the joint findings of research-oriented and practical studies. They only evolved after appropriate theories of group functioning were established and they were developed alongside these developing theories. Unfortunately, many users of group dynamics seem to have forgotten the essential link which has always operated in the development of group dynamics — the link between theory and research and practice. Modern T-group users, particularly those in more esoteric areas, often resist analyses being made of the ways such groups function on the basis that such analyses might destroy the essential ethos of the group. If it is such a fragile thing — which I take leave to doubt — then the T-group can hardly be accepted as a useful tool for the social scientist concerned with the harsh realities of life.

A more serious problem, however, may be discerned in the emphasis on total personality involvement which of itself, it is argued, will lead to growth. In many T-group sessions no guidance is given to direct the interaction flow. In some cases this has led to a session of silence. In others it has led to more forceful members monopolizing the interaction, directing it where they will. We must not forget that Lewin spoke always of planned change and saw the group's force as being to foster directional change for community development. Sometimes we are in danger now of simply setting up powerful forces for unplanned change, change which is haphazard and may be destructive. It is better to regard the T-group not as a task free group but one whose task is inner directed, whose goal is enhancement of the group members, the group itself, and possibly the community from which the group comes. What is required is *not* a leaderless group but a group with strong socio-leaders in Bales' (1958) sense. Any developmental psychologist knows that uncontrolled emotional experiences lead not to growth but breakdown. The T-group if uncontrolled can bring enormous pressures to bear on the individual member. Emotional expression may be catharctic or self-reinforcing according to circumstances and in the total personality T-group too quick a breakdown of barriers can lead to the too early display of deep emotions with consequent behaviour breakdown. The group — any group — is a powerful moulding force on behaviour. T-groups offer a seemingly simple and powerful tool to the social scientist. A knowledge of the history of group studies, a knowledge of general social group functioning, however, would indicate caution. Groups influence their members' behaviours in complex ways. Only careful group manipulation can restrict these influences towards positive growth.

An Appraisal of the Airline Pilot Selection Scheme

The methods and techniques which I have described in this book were put into practice in the selection of airline pilots. The selection scheme for pilots has been described in Chapter 8, where the time-table of the selection is given. At this stage it should be useful to the reader to give a detailed appraisal of the scheme in operation. This appendix is concerned with the pilot selection scheme and describes the values and limits of the various parts of the procedure.

Firstly, it is of interest to see to what extent the various parts of the procedure contributed towards the final result as expressed in the decision made by the Final Selection Board. One possibility, of course, is that the Final Selection Board only paid "lip service" to using the assessments made on various parts of the selection procedure and in fact still made its decision on its own foreshortened Board Interview. Another possibility is that the Flight Manager's interview was being given exclusive attention and the other measures ignored, on the unstated assumption that the Flight Manager as a pilot himself would know better! That neither of these possibilities occurred in practice can be seen from Table A.1, which shows the biserial correlations between the various parts of the selection procedure and the Final Selection Board's decision. It can be seen from this table that both interviews correlate highly with the F.S.B.'s decision as does the rating from the Group Exercises. These three parts of the procedure each play an important part in the making of the final decision. Nor is the Flight Manager's

TABLE A.1. *The biserial correlations between the various
selection assessments in the pilot selection programme and the
Final Selection Board's decisions*

Selection measure	Biserial r with F.S.B.
(1) Progressive matrices, 1938	0.127
(2) Scientific aptitude test	0.059
(3) General knowledge	0.128
(4) Mathematics test	0.174
(items 1 to 4 were paper and pencil aptitude tests)	
(5) Psychologist's interview	0.594
(6) Flight Manager's interview	0.621
(7) Group Exercises, overall rating	0.706
(assessments from two observers combined)	

Based on N=200 cases, when r must be 0.153 to reach 0.05 level of
significance and r must be 0.190 to reach 0.01 level of significance.

semi-technical interview rating used by the F.S.B. to any
significantly greater extent than the psychologist's general
personality interview. The weight given to the various parts
seems fairly distributed and the obtained difference between
correlations contrasting the F.S.B. and the two interviews on
the one hand and the Group Exercises on the other is probably
due to the following two factors. Firstly, the interviews come
first chronologically, when the candidate is not so settled and
when little is known about him. Secondly, the Combined Group
Exercise rating averages out the views of the two major
assessors. This in itself would naturally lead to a more
noteworthy rating, and in addition by the time the assessors
came to make their final group rating they had seen the
candidates for nearly 2 days. Thus, in spite of the fact that the
instructions given to the assessors were to treat independently
each assessment, there is no doubt that the group exercise
assessment was in some slight degree affected by the assessors'
general overview of the candidate.

One further interesting finding arises from Table A.1. As I

mentioned earlier (Chapter 8), paper-and-pencil aptitude tests were used at first. The correlations between these tests and the F.S.B. all fail to reach a significant level with the exception of mathematics, which is just significant at the 0.05 level. Apart from their practical implications, these results also suggest that there is essentially a dissimilarity between assessments made from formal, objective tests and those made from interviews which are dynamic interaction processes.

The analysis can be taken further if multiple correlations for each stage of the selection procedure are computed, using the Final Selection Board's decision as a criterion. The multiple R's for all variables and pairs of assessments, correlated with F.S.B. results, can be seen in Table A.2. From this table it can be seen that in arriving at a decision the F.S.B. did not give equal weight to all three assessments. In fact, greatest reliance was placed on the combined assessment from the Group Exercises and the psychologist's interview. If nothing else, this suggests that the new selection method had gained acceptance. More important, it suggests too that it was the personality elements rather than the technical ones which were the ruling factors in selection.

As well as the relationship of each variable to the F.S.B. result, the various relationships between assessments were calculated and as these are of interest in themselves, they are

TABLE A.2. *Multiple correlations between various combinations of assessments and Final Selection Board's decision*

Combination of assessments	Multiple R with F.S.B.
(1) Psychologist's+Flight Manager's interviews	0.659
(2) Psychologist's interview+Group Exercise rating	0.901
(3) Flight Manager's interview+Group Exercise rating	0.727
(4) All three variables	0.765

shown in Table A.3. As is to be expected, it can be seen that the correlation between the two interviews is relatively high. Although the two interviewers had different tasks, the Flight Manager had been instructed briefly in interviewing techniques and was conducting a biographical free interview much along the lines suggested in this book. Thus in spite of his task of assessing the candidate's ability to think in terms of technical aviation concepts, he was also succeeding, it would seem, in making a more general personality assessment.

Both interviews are correlated with the Group Exercise overall combined rating to about the same degree. The Group Exercises, though overlapping to some extent with the interviews, yet seem to measure much that is different. This confirms the theoretical supposition that as well as providing the basis for a general personality assessment through the opportunity to observe people "doing things", the opportunity to observe them as "going wholes", group interviews also provide a measure of something more, the leadership factor.

The Reliability of the Procedure

So far, as a measure of performance in the Group Exercises, I have used the combined overall rating. This combined rating was produced by taking the average of the two overall assessments of the two assessors rating any one group. This combined rating is most useful in assessing the relationship of the Group Exercises as such to other measures, since to a

TABLE A.3. *Inter correlations between pairs of assessment variables*

	Psychologist's interview	Flight Manager's interview
Flight Manager's Interview	0.708	—
Combined Assessment from Group Exercises	0.608	0.593

certain extent by combining ratings it balances out the effect of differing standards of individual assessors. By taking the separate ratings of a pair of assessors on a group of candidates, however, we can obtain essential information as to the reliability of the trait-rating methods. One of the criticisms of all interviews, it will be remembered, is that being relatively unstandardized they are generally unreliable. The technique of isolating traits and then rating candidates on these was suggested to help overcome the problem of reliability, and it is interesting to see if it has succeeded.

In the Pilot Selection Programme candidates were seen in groups of six or seven. Each group was observed by two assessors who rated all the candidates on each of the thirteen traits referred to in Table 8.2. That ratings are used and not rankings overcomes the problem of comparing results between groups, to some extent at least. The observers had to make an absolute judgement on a given scale (see p. 93) and were not merely saying "This is the best in such-and-such a quality in this group". Thus, I would suggest that it can be assumed that the reliability coefficients represent reliability of comparisons of individuals from different groups.

The results, shown in Table A.4, are taken from 200 candidates where in 75% of the cases ratings were made by myself and the senior Flight Manager. In the other 25% of the cases this Flight Manager and one other did the rating. It can be argued that since these observers were trained by me, this would enhance the chances of getting agreement. This I think is so, but the fact that the coefficients represent ratings made at different times by four different observers should act in the opposite direction and reduce the probability of getting high agreement.

That the method I have suggested for controlling the assessment of candidates in group interviews is reasonably successful can be seen from the average inter-trait reliability coefficient which is 0.85 and from the overall rating on "Command Potential", the extent to which the candidate's performance on the Group Exercises as a whole showed leadership potential for this situation, which is 0.94. Some of

138 Assessment through Interviewing

the individual traits are not so reliably assessed, suggesting that the observers were less clear about the meaning of these, but on the whole, even keeping in mind the effects of common training of the assessors, these ratings show reliabilities about comparable with standardized tests.

Studies of Validity

I have reported fully the validatory work carried out on the Pilot Selection Procedure elsewhere (Shouksmith, 1960b) and pointed out that one of the difficulties in following up most selection work is to find a criterion against which predictions may be judged. This is particularly so where an attempt is being made to predict "leadership" or "command" qualities. In follow-up studies of the Pilot Selection Procedure, three separate criteria were used in three approaches to the problem.

The first and simplest was a "wastage" figure, which showed that over the training period of six months and a further six months line flying, the total wastage from all sources was 4% or

TABLE A.4. *Reliability of trait rating method of assessment of group interactions, as measured by the correlations obtained for ratings of same candidates made by two observers*

Inspires confidence	0.89
Dependability	0.79
Initiative	0.90
Keenness	0.85
Calmness	0.85
Self-discipline	0.86
Appearance and bearing	0.89
Decisiveness	0.93
Adaptability	0.83
Co-operation	0.75
Commands respect	0.88
Sense of humour	0.77
Breadth of outlook	0.86
Average of above individual coefficients	0.85
Overall rating on "Command Potential"	0.94

An Appraisal of the Selection Scheme   139

in effect two pilots. This compared with over 12% wastage on previous intakes during a similar period. There are, however, two major disadvantages of using wastage as a criterion. Firstly, wastage over 12 months is hardly adequate when we are concerned with Command Potential, and secondly no conclusions as to the individual merits and demerits of those chosen can be made and the findings cannot therefore be used for improving further selections.

The second criterion used was an attempted rating on training which proved to be useless as instructors were unwilling to differentiate among trainees who had passed through the training school. Training was carried out to a certain standard, they argued, and all that they could say was whether a pilot came up to that standard or not. Since, if he failed to come up to their standard, his contract was not made permanent, those of unsatisfactory standard would appear in the wastage figure anyway.

For the third approach, I produced what might be called a "disguised" rating scale. Through the "conference" method of group discussions, carried out with all the Flight Managers, a number of verbal descriptions of "good", "bad", and "indifferent" pilots and captains was established. These were allied to five categories which formed the rating scale given below:

The "Criterion Categories"

(1) Good, a first-class man both in and out of the cockpit: should make a markedly above average Corporation pilot.

(2) Competent plus, a man you would choose to take with you as First Officer.

(3) Competent and adequate: no outstanding features but a reasonable First Officer.

(4) A man who, although acceptable to you as a pilot, has one or two features which are unsatisfactory: as a First Officer he does his job, but you are not always happy with him.

(5) Not really up to the standard of flying, technical ability or behaviour required of the Corporation's pilots.

The Flight Managers of the Corporation were then asked to judge trainees in their respective commands in terms of the verbal descriptions they themselves had produced in discussions, and assign trainees to the appropriate categories. By using this method, each person doing the rating had been involved in setting up the categories and so was identified with them, and furthermore, each one had discussed the matter fully enough to have a real idea of what each category meant to his colleagues and fellow raters. This follow-up was carried out on pilots during the period eighteen months to two years after their appointment. Correlation coefficients are not very meaningful with such a highly selected group, but, for what it is worth, these ratings correlated 0.51 with the initial Selection Board grades, which figure compares well with previous findings of similar selection techniques.

A Factorial Analysis of the Procedure

The results from the two interviews and the twelve major trait ratings were intercorrelated and submitted to a principal components factor analysis, the results of which appear in Table A.5.

Identifying the Factors

Factor F1

This factor has its only truly significant loadings on the two interviews and hence must be regarded as an "interview" factor. Its psychological meaning can best be understood through considering the interview tasks. The area of overlap seems to be in the search for emotional stability. The psychologist's interview was in part concerned with picking out the stable,

TABLE A.5. *Rotated factor matrix showing significant loadings only for Pilot Selection Procedure* (decimal point omitted from table)

Variable	Factor loadings			
	F1	F2	F3	h^2
(1) Psychologist's interview	84			71
(2) Flight Manager's interview	74		21	59
(3) Breadth of outlook		55	64	72
(4) Clarity of thinking		70	43	67
(5) Decisiveness		76	50	76
(6) Inspires confidence		38	75	72
(7) Co-operation		68	36	59
(8) Calmness		70	28	56
(9) Appearance and bearing			82	70
(10) Sense of humour	21	28	76	71
(11) Keenness	28	43	31	37
(12) Dependability		88		80
(13) Commands respect		90		85
(14) Self-discipline	21	78		66

controlled individual who would not be likely to crack under stress. As regards the Flight Manager's interview one would assume some overlap, since although concerned with technical aspects, the candidate's personality would naturally enter into the picture. The best way of interpreting this factor seems to be in a general way as general emotional stability. This matches with what Cattell has identified as his factor C, "emotional stability or ego strength". The person who is high in factor C is emotionally mature, says Cattell (1957), emotionally stable, calm, phlegmatic, realistic about life and interestingly enough is usually found in jobs requiring adjustment to difficulties thrown up from outside.

Factor F2

This factor depends for its identity on major loadings in

"dependability", "commands respect", "self-discipline", and to a lesser extent "decisiveness". The best definition one can give to this factor is that it measures "solid worth" or what Cattell calls "praxernia" and links with the practical person who is concerned with facts. The praxernic person tends to be conventional, but is alert to practical needs and shows a sound and realistic practical judgement. The factor as it is isolated here suggests essentially "the practical man", who may not be an ideas man, but one who can use ideas and put them into practice.

Factor F3

This final factor loads essentially on "sense of humour", "breadth of outlook", "inspires confidence", and "appearance and bearing", with slightly lower loadings on "clarity of thinking" and "decisiveness". Thus I define this one — though perhaps more tentatively than the others — as extroversion. Extroversion can be of many sorts and in this particular case would seem to be what is usually referred to as "thinking extroversion". The person loading highly on this one is not merely a social extrovert but is a rounded sort of person who acts in an outgoing, extrovertive way on a basis of the results of his serious thinking rather than merely on whim.

Bibliography

Allport, Gordon W. (1937) *Personality: A Psychological Interpretation.* New York: Holt & Co.

Anstey, E, and Mercer, E. O. (1956) *Interviewing for the Selection of Staff.* London: George Allen & Unwin.

Arbous, A. G. (1953) *Selection for Industrial Leadership.* London: Oxford University Press.

Arbuckle, D. S. (1961) *Counselling: An Introduction.* Boston: Allyn & Bacon Inc.

Bach, G. (1954) *Intensive Group Psychotherapy.* New York: Ronald Press.

Bales, R. F. (1950) *Interaction Process Analysis: A Method for the Study of Small Groups.* Reading, Mass: Addison Wesley.

Bales, R. F. (1958) Task roles and social roles in problem solving groups, in MacCoby, E. E., Newcomb, T. M., and Hartley, F. L. (eds.) *Readings in Social Psychology* (3rd ed.). New York: Holt, Rinehart & Winston.

Bass, B. M. (1968) Interface between personnel and organizational psychology. *J. Applied Psychol.* 52, 81–88.

Bass, B. M. and Norton, F. T. M. (1951) Group size and leaderless discussion. *J. Applied Psychol.* 35, 397–400.

Bellows, R. (1961) *Psychology of Personnel in Business and Industry,* 3rd ed. Englewood Cliffs, N.J.: Prentice-Hall.

Benne, K. D. and Sheats, P. (1948) Functional roles of group members. *J. Social Issues* 2, 42–47.

Bennis, W. G., Benne, K. D., and Chin, R. (eds.) (1961) *The Planning of Change.* New York: Holt, Rinehart & Winston.

Bingham, W. Van Dyke and Moore, B. V. (1959) *How to Interview,* 4th ed. New York: Harper Bros.

Bion, W. R. (1948) *Experiences in Groups, Human Relations,* 1, 314–20 and 487–96.

Brammer, L. M. (1973) *The Helping Relationship* Englewood Cliffs, N.J.: Prentice-Hall.

Brammer, L. M. and Shostrom, E. L. (1960) *Therapeutic Psychology.* Englewood Cliffs, N.J.: Prentice-Hall.

143

Burgoon, M., Heston, J. K., and McCroskey, J. (1974) *Small Group Communication: A Functional Approach.* New York: Holt, Rinehart & Winston.

Burt, Sir C. (1925) *The Young Delinquent.* London: University of London Press.

Carkhuff, R. (1969) *Helping and Human Relations.* New York: Holt, Rinehart & Winston.

Carlson, R. E., Thayer, P. W., Mayfield, E. C., and Petersen, D. A. (1971) Improvements in the selection interview. *Personnel Journal* 50, 268–75.

Cattel, R. B. (1957) *Personality and Motivation Structure and Measurement.* New York: World Book Co.

Cooley, C. S. (1909) *Social Organization.* New York: Scribner.

Eysenck, H. J. (1952) The effects of psychotherapy: an evaluation. *J. Consulting Psychol.* 16, 319–24.

Flanagan, J. (1947) Critical requirements, in Dennis, W. (ed.)., *Current Trends in Industrial Psychology.* Pittsburgh: University of Pittsburg Press.

Fraser, J. M. (1950) New type selection boards: a further communication. *Occup. Psychol.* 24, 40–47.

Ginzberg, E. S. W., Ginsburg, S. Axelrad, and Herma, J. L. (1951) *Occupational Choice: An Approach to a General Theory.* New York: Columbia University Press.

Grant, D. L and Bray, D. (1969) Contributions of the interview to assessment of management potential. *J. Applied Psychol.* 53, 24–34.

Hahn, M. E. and MacLean, M. S. (1955) *Counselling Psychology.* New York: McGraw-Hill.

Hepner, H. W. (1951) *Psychology Applied to Life and Work.* Englewood Cliffs, N.J.: Prentice-Hall.

Hill, W. F. (1973) Hill Interaction Matrix (HIM) conceptual framework for understanding groups, in Jones, J. E. and Pfeiffer, J. W. (eds.), *The 1973 Annual Handbook for Group Facilitators.* Iowa City, Iowa: University Associates.

Hollingworth, H. L. (1929) *Vocational Psychology and Character Analysis.* New York: D. Appleton & Co.

Homans, George C. (1958) Social behaviour as exchange. *Am. J. Sociol.* 63, (6) 597–606.

Hoppock, R. (1957) *Occupational Information.* New York: McGraw-Hill.

Hunt, W. A., Watson, C. L. and Harris, H. L. (1944) The screen test in military selection. *Psychol. Review* 51, 37–46.

Ivey, A. E. (1971) *Microcounselling.* Springfield, Ill.: Charles C. Thomas.

Johnson, P. W. (1972) *Reaching Out.* Englewood Cliffs, N.J.: Prentice-Hall.

Johnson, W. J. and Shouksmith, G. A. (1956) *Report on the Pilot Selection Procedure.* B.E.A. Technical Report.

Kelly, E. and Fiske, D. (1951) *The Prediction of Performance in Clinical Psychology.* Ann Arbor: University of Michigan Press.

Laird, D. (1937) *Psychology of Selecting Employees.* New York: McGraw-Hill.

Lewin, K. (1947) Frontiers in group dynamics: II, Channels of group life: social planning and action research. *Human Relations* 1, 143—53.

Maier, N. R. E. (1958) *The Appraisal Interview: Objectives, Methods, and Skills.* New York: John Wiley.

Mills, T. M. (1967) *Group Transformation.* Englewood Cliffs, N.J.: Prentice-Hall.

Morris, Ben S. (1949) Officer selection in the British Army. *Occup. Psychol.* 23, 219—34.

Newman, J. W. (1957) *Motivation Research and Marketing Management.* Boston: Harvard University Graduate School of Business Administration, Division of Research.

Oldfield, R. C. (1941) *The Psychology of the Interview.* London: Methuen.

Rodger, A. (1952) *The Seven Point Plan.* N.I.I.P. Paper No. 1, 1952.

Roethlisberger, F. J. and Dickson, W. J. (1950) *Management and the Worker,* 10th Printing. Cambridge, Mass.: Harvard University Press.

Rogers, Carl R. (1942) *Counseling and Psychotherapy.* Cambridge, Mass.: The Houghton Mifflin Co.

Sarbin, T. R. (1954) In Lindzey, G. (ed.), *Handbook of Social Psychology.* Cambridge, Mass.: Addison-Wesley.

Schein, E. H. (1969) *Process Consultation: Its Role in Organizational Development.* Reading, Mass.: Addison-Wesley.

Shouksmith, G. (1958) Command qualities in airline pilots. *Austr. J. Psychol.* 10 (3), 351—6.

Shouksmith, G. (1960a) Developing clinical psychology in New Zealand. *Mental Hospitals* 11 (9).

Shouksmith, G. (1960b) A validatory criterion for a group selection procedure *Austr. J. Psychol.* 12 (1), 33—39.

Smith, H. C. (1973) *Sensitivity Training.* New York: McGraw-Hill.

Stogdill, R. M. (1942) Personal factors associated with leadership: a review of the literature. *J. Psychol.* 25, 35—67.

Symonds, P. M. (1939) Research on the interviewing process. *J. Educ. Psychol.* 30, 346—53.

Thibaut, J. W. and Kelley, H. W. (1959) *The Social Psychology of Groups.* New York: John Wiley.

Vernon, P. E. (1950) The validation of civil service selection boards. *Occup. Psychol.* 24, 75—95.

Vernon, P. E. and Parry, J. B. (1949) *Personnel Selection in the British Forces.* London: Univ. of London Press.

Walton, H. (ed.) (1971) *Small Group Psychotherapy.* Harmondsworth, Middx.: Penguin Books.

Wilson, N. A. B. (1948) The work of C.S.S.B. *Occup. Psychol.* 22, 204—12.

Index

147

148   *Index*